More Praise for *Making Questions Work*

"A powerful and practical book of guidelines, tips, and options for anyone who does facilitation and wants to learn and apply the skill of asking the right questions of the right people at the right time. This is a facilitation bible, a 'must-have' for thoughtful planning and addressing facilitation challenges."

—Nancy Lalonde, director of organizational development,
University of Ottawa, Canada

"For public-policy advocates and other such issue-strategists, *Making Questions Work* is a valuable exploration tool in the never-ending search for the solutions, compromises, and agreements that are the stuff of government and community decision making."

—Sean Moore, partner and public policy advisor,
Gowling Lefleur Henderson LLP, Ottawa, Canada

"If you design and facilitate workshops and meetings, you need this book in your library. This is not a book to read once; this is a valuable resource to return to over and over again. Whether you are a workshop facilitator or facilitative leader, Dorothy Strachan's knowledge, experience, and insights will improve your meeting designs and save you time."

—Brian Benn, regional manager,
Centre for Leadership and Learning, Province of Ontario, Canada

"Whether you are a coach, trainer, facilitator, or leader, if you believe in the power of questions to inspire and transform people, *Making Questions Work* is the ultimate reference guide. The great thing about Dorothy Strachan's book is that every time I pick it up I find new insights and new ways to craft questions."

—Pierre-Claude Elie, change facilitator,
Emergence Solutions Inc., Montreal, Canada

"Dorothy Strachan brings immense practical experience and tremendous insight into building teams and facilitating groups with her book *Making Questions Work*. This is an invaluable resource for anyone striving to help a group work together more effectively and perform at a higher level."

—John Bales, chief executive officer, Coaching Association of Canada

"The ability to ask questions effectively is critical for me as a professional facilitator. I am thrilled to have a handbook that puts the emphasis on something so important to both my work and personal life. Thank you, Dorothy Strachan, for this terrific resource!"

—Carol Lauder, grant project manager, Texas Comptroller's Office

JB JOSSEY-BASS

MAKING QUESTIONS WORK

A Guide to What and How to Ask
for Facilitators, Consultants,
Managers, Coaches, and Educators

·DOROTHY STRACHAN

BICENTENNIAL
1807
WILEY
2007
BICENTENNIAL

John Wiley & Sons, Inc.

Published by Jossey-Bass
A Wiley Imprint
989 Market Street, San Francisco, CA 94103-1741   www.josseybass.com

Jossey-Bass books and products are available through most bookstores. To contact Jossey-Bass directly call our Customer Care Department within the U.S. at 800-956-7739, outside the U.S. at 317-572-3986, or fax 317-572-4002.

Jossey-Bass also publishes its books in a variety of electronic formats. Some content that appears in print may not be available in electronic books.

Library of Congress Cataloging-in-Publication Data

Strachan, Dorothy, date.
  Making questions work: a guide to what and how to ask for facilitators, consultants, managers, coaches, and educators / Dorothy Strachan.
      p. cm.
   ISBN-13: 978-0-7879-8727-5
   ISBN-10: 0-7879-8727-1
1. Group facilitation. 2. Problem solving.
3. Questioning. 4. Critical thinking. I. Title.
   HM751.S77 2007
   658.3'14—dc22   2006028743

Printed in the United States of America
FIRST EDITION
PB Printing   10 9 8 7 6 5 4 3 2

The Jossey-Bass Business and Management Series

Contents

PART ONE

HOW TO ASK QUESTIONS

For my family, who have weathered (often without complaint)
so many, many questions over the years.
I will continue to try to improve on our golden dictum:
"No questions after 9:00 P.M."

Acknowledgments

Many colleagues, clients, and process participants, both as individuals and as groups, have contributed in their own special way to this book. A sincere thank-you to all who have been part of a wonderful writing process over the past several years.

Special thanks go to Paul Tomlinson and Marian Pitters for their thoughtful and comprehensive reviews of early drafts; all those who contributed to an earlier version of this book, titled *Questions That Work*; and Ana Ruiz, for her patient and steadfast administrative support.

The Author

Dorothy Strachan is a partner in Strachan-Tomlinson, an Ottawa-based process consulting firm. Prior to founding Strachan-Tomlinson, she was involved in high school and community college education as a teacher and administrator. She has been working as a full-time process consultant and professional facilitator since 1974, serving clients across the public, nonprofit, and private sectors in several countries.

In addition to her consulting work, Strachan spends considerable time creating and delivering learning-centered training sessions in her field. Participants in her workshops on process design, facilitation, and dynamic questioning typically describe them as practical and immediately usable learning experiences.

Strachan is the author of several books and handbooks that focus on processes for leadership development, facilitation, workshop management, effective coaching in high-performance sports, working with volunteers, and strategic planning. (For more information, visit www.strachan-tomlinson.com.) A number of these publications reflect Strachan-Tomlinson's special interest in health policy at all levels, from community-based organizations to national and international alliances.

Preface

Being a facilitator has consumed a good part of my life. I started out as a high school teacher and then moved into the community college system as a teacher and administrator, before venturing into professional facilitation as a principal in a small consulting firm.

Today I am a partner in Strachan-Tomlinson, an Ottawa-based process consulting firm. A large part of what we have been doing for the past thirty years focuses on design and facilitation of organizational processes in areas such as strategic planning, team development, policy development, knowledge translation, organizational change, and training for facilitators and process consultants. We work with a variety of clients in the public, private, and not-for-profit sectors in local, regional, national, and international settings.

My business partner is Paul Tomlinson. Paul's primary expertise is in gathering and developing the background information and concepts that inform our facilitation efforts. His background in adult education has been an important element in building our company's learning-centered approach to group process and organizational change. The *we* in this book refers to Paul and me.

October 2006   Dorothy Strachan
Ottawa, Canada

Introduction

Most facilitators spend considerable time looking for and thinking about questions for a particular topic in a particular situation with a particular group of people. Some questions work brilliantly with one group and not at all with another.

This book reduces the amount of effort and time required to find or develop these questions. The focus is on basic frameworks; on practical, proven, adaptable tools; and on a wealth of specific strategies and examples.

This resource is designed for facilitators who have some experience working with groups and are interested in expanding their knowledge and expertise about how to make questions work well. This includes professional facilitators as well as managers, teachers, trainers, community organizers, project leaders, lawyers, executives, professors, health care professionals, mediators, negotiators, human resources professionals, politicians, coaches, social workers, and counselors. Many people do facilitation as a regular part of their work and yet don't think of themselves as professional facilitators; this resource is also for them.

Regardless of your role, the right questions for the right people at the right time are at the heart of healthy group process—a top priority in effective and dynamic facilitation.

Making Questions Work is filled with hundreds of practice guidelines, tips, and suggestions for facilitators.

Part One, "How to Ask Questions," explores some basic parameters for effective questioning.

Chapter One, "Questions That Work," describes process frameworks for questions, how to construct questions, question types, conscious questioning skills, and some dos and don'ts.

Chapter Two, "Core Facilitation Values," explores how your values guide the use of questions in support of healthy group process.

Chapter Three, "Follow-up Questions," outlines a range of prompts to support deeper discussion.

In Part Two, "What to Ask When," five chapters present some eighteen hundred sample questions that enable facilitators to meet common challenges with groups. Although each chapter is designed to stand on its own, it is also interrelated with the others. For example, the values described in Chapter Two are at the heart of what makes the framework in Chapter Four (on opening questions) work well, and the questions in Chapter Six (on critical thinking) may also be used to supplement the framework for addressing issues in Chapter Seven.

Nuance and context are the key. Although more than one chapter has questions focused on taking action, the questions in Chapter Five on this topic are for a context different from those in Chapter Seven. Getting the nuance appropriate to the context is what makes a question specific to a situation.

Each chapter in Part Two begins with a process framework, which acts as a general map of facilitation challenges for that chapter's topic. This is followed by guidelines for developing and using questions and lists of questions divided into focus areas. Space is provided for you to write down additional questions so that you can make this handbook into a personalized question bank. At the end of each chapter, common challenges that facilitators face are presented as brief case studies.

Chapter Four, "Questions for Opening a Session," outlines a process framework for participants to get to know one another, clarify expectations, and build commitment.

Chapter Five, "Questions for Enabling Action," describes the "What?—So what?—Now what?" process framework, a three-step approach to outcomes-based facilitating.

Chapter Six, "Questions for Thinking Critically," helps participants reflect on how and why things are done the way they are, an important skill for complex problem solving in groups.

Chapter Seven, "Questions for Addressing Issues," lays out a systematic approach to six areas of inquiry related to issues analysis and management, a common element in many facilitated processes.

Chapter Eight, "Questions for Closing a Session," includes a variety of options for challenges that facilitators face in concluding a process.

"In Closing: About Questions—What I Know for Sure" describes insights that are based on many years as a process consultant in a range of situations.

A QUICK LOOKUP RESOURCE

The Contents for this book is also the index. Skim the headings in the Contents to search for the type of session and question you want. Then go to that page and peruse the list of sample questions.

If you want to find a chapter quickly, hold the book in your left hand with the cover face down and put your thumb on the related chapter tab on the back cover. Thumb through the pages until you get to the matching gray strip for that chapter.

ABOUT WORDS

Here we explain what we mean by several words used frequently throughout this book.

- *Client:* The client is the person or group of persons with whom the process is developed and to whom the facilitator is accountable. The client may be a planning committee, an administrator, a board of directors, a manager, or another responsible person or group.
- *Facilitator:* A facilitator is someone who attends to group process. This includes professional facilitators as well as managers, teachers, trainers, community organizers, project leaders, lawyers, executives, professors, health care professionals, mediators, negotiators, human resource professionals, politicians, social workers, and counselors. Many people do facilitation as a regular part of their work and yet don't think of themselves as professional facilitators.

- *Group:* Three or more people who want to accomplish something.
- *Group members:* Participants in a group process; this phrase is used interchangeably with *participants.*
- *Participants:* People who are participating in a group process; this word is used interchangeably with *group members.*
- *Plenary:* When all members of an assembly are present; for example, when a number of small groups are together in a meeting of the whole group.
- *Process:* A structured group experience; a process may happen in a variety of settings (work session, workshop, meeting, conference, roundtable).
- *Prompt:* A follow-up question designed to clarify a response or to get more information in a specific area.
- *Session:* A facilitated process that happens in a limited time period—a few hours, a day, a weekend, a week; may also be called a workshop, meeting, or conference.

By presenting what works for us, we hope that you will find some practical ideas and tools for asking people the right questions at the right time.

MAKING QUESTIONS WORK

HOW TO ASK
QUESTIONS

1

Questions That Work

When it comes to facilitation, questions make things happen; they are the engine that drives healthy and productive group processes.

Facilitators develop questions in response to facilitation challenges. The right question is the one that works best at a particular moment in a particular situation with a particular group of people. Sometimes a question works brilliantly with one group and not at all with another—context is critical.

Questions work when they contribute to the purpose and objectives of a process. In the hands of a skilled facilitator, effective questions are the foundation for such activities as opening a session, building consensus for decision making, enabling action, thinking critically, addressing issues, and closing a session.

A few years ago, a national think tank brought together Canada's "top thirty" corporate chief executive officers to create a national strategy to develop and support up-and-coming young leaders in business. As part of the opening session, we asked participants to introduce themselves by answering the question, "What is an important learning you have had about organizational leadership in your working life? Please answer in the form of a commandment."

Responses to this question were varied, rich, and concise. They energized the group, focused the discussion on what new business leaders need to learn, encouraged risk taking, generated new ideas, and initiated development of a national leadership vision.

1

Participants said things such as:

- Enable people to mourn the past so that they can change in the future.

- Build on the organization's legacy and traditions.

- Get the organization change-ready.

- Lead *toward* something, not away from something.

- Organizational leadership takes passion and big steps; leadership is not a spectator sport.

- Political and business leadership do not always go in the same direction.

Watching these responses work their magic with that group was a satisfying experience. Questions have not worked as well during other introductions, for a variety of reasons; perhaps they weren't focused enough, or they confronted participants too much or too little. At other times, in writing a final report we have discovered that a session might have been considerably more productive if we had just tweaked a few questions during small group discussions so that they directed participants more clearly toward a specific outcome.

When questions really work, you can almost see them sweating to support the process and enable participants to get where they want to go.

PROCESS FRAMEWORKS

A process framework is a step-by-step conceptual guide to what a facilitator does in a structured group experience.

It is like a map organized around facilitation challenges. It makes the process explicit, furnishes a reference point for keeping a process on track, and supports facilitators in thinking about questions consciously, whether for a single workshop on strategic planning or a long-term, multisession team development initiative.

Although all processes have their own unique history, situation, objectives, and complicating factors, they also share typical facilitation challenges. Five process frameworks (Figure 1.1) for common facilitation challenges are found in Part Two of this book.

Opening a Session	Enabling Action	Thinking Critically	Addressing Issues	Closing a Session
1. Getting to know one another	1. What? (Observation)	1. Making assumptions and perspectives explicit	1. Understanding the situation	1. Looking backward: wrapping up the process
2. Clarifying expectations	2. So what? (Reflection)	2. Understanding interests and power relationships	2. Clarifying the issues	2. Looking forward: considering next steps
3. Building commitment	3. Now what? (Action)	3. Exploring alternative ways of thinking and acting	3. Generating options for action	
		4. Making ethical choices	4. Testing options for action	
			5. Making a decision	
			6. Taking action	

Figure 1.1. Five Process Frameworks.

1

> One way of looking at the world as a whole is by means of a map, that is to say, some sort of a plan or outline that shows where various things are to be found—not all things, of course, for that would make the map as big as the world, but the things that are most prominent, most important for orientation—outstanding landmarks, as it were, which you cannot miss, or if you do miss, you will be left in total perplexity.
>
> —*Schumacher, 1977*

Process frameworks offer a concrete approach to a facilitation challenge. Most sessions use a minimum of three frameworks—one to open the process, one to address a specific challenge, and one to close the process. Once you are clear about the framework or combination of frameworks required for a process, the questions you need will become obvious by looking at the key parts of the framework: they enable you to make conscious decisions about what to ask to accomplish your objectives.

For example, if you are facilitating a group to move toward specific action based on recommendations in a report, you can use the process framework for enabling action (Figure 1.2, and Chapter Five) to guide how you think about the questions required.

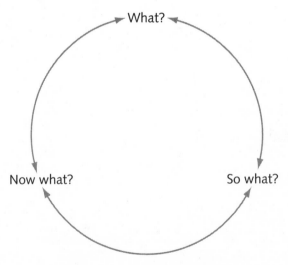

Figure 1.2. Process Framework for Enabling Action.

On the basis of this process framework, at some point in the session you will be paying close attention to questions in the "now what" section that help drive the process toward decision mak-

> *Learn and lean on your process frameworks; don't leave home without them.*

ing. These questions may be developed ahead of time, or you might make them up on the spot. Either way, it is the process framework that helps you consciously shape the questions required to enable the group to move forward.

Process frameworks are flexible. Just as a map is not the territory, so a framework is not the process. However, it is a strong reference point and suggests a basic structure, which is what makes it useful (Korzybski, 1933). Instead of a facilitator feeling stuck in a session and wondering what she should ask next, she leans on the process framework for the kind of question she needs, thinking, "We've spent enough time discussing what stands out in this report; they probably need to move on to the reflection part of the framework." In this way, a process framework is a reference point for questions that fit a specific situation. For example, if you want to encourage critical reflection (see Figure 1.3), lean on the process framework in Chapter Six to guide how you develop and use questions.

If you notice that people need more time to make their assumptions and perspectives explicit than what you have allotted on the agenda, you might decide to spend an additional twenty or thirty minutes using questions that you create on the spot to clarify perspectives further.

A process framework both requires and enables facilitators to take a participant-observer stance. In this stance, the facilitator functions in a dual role, attending to both content and process, noticing how questions

> You can tell whether a man is clever by his answers. You can tell whether a man is wise by his questions.
>
> —Naguib Mahfouz, 1988

are working and also making decisions about what to ask next (see Chapter Two).

Just as it takes a lot of experience to become a skilled navigator in the wilderness, it also takes a lot of facilitation experience to become a skilled participant-observer in a group. This involves using a process framework to guide a session, tracking group process, noting stages of group development, and intervening when appropriate to achieve objectives.

1

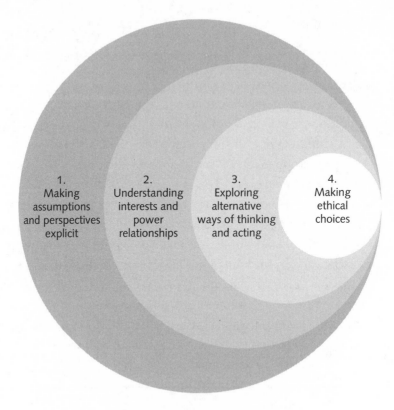

Figure 1.3. Process Framework for Thinking Critically.

CONSCIOUS QUESTIONING

Questions that work have intention; they enable a group to get where it wants to go. They are created deliberately to support achievement of the purpose and objectives of a process and are situated within a process framework that guides participants toward expected outcomes.

To create effective questions that have meaning in a specific context and process, facilitators need to know:

- The purpose and objectives of the process

- The situation and related facilitation challenges

- The people involved

- The process frameworks required to address the facilitation challenges

- Themselves

Conscious questioning is based on clear intention and comprehensive preparation. It includes time spent learning about your client, the organization, the situation, and the participants. It can also involve reviewing background documents, interviewing people, summarizing main issues, and researching recent publications. The final challenge—knowing yourself as a facilitator—is grounded in how you understand and apply your core values, as described in Chapter Two.

Framing Questions

There are many ways to frame questions. For example, *Bloom's taxonomy* is based on six categories: knowledge, comprehension, application, analysis, synthesis, and evaluation (Bloom, 1956). The *focused conversation* approach has four levels of questions: objective, reflective, interpretive, and decisional (Stanfield, 2000a). The *critical thinking community* talks about three types: those with a right answer, those with better or worse answers, and those with as many answers as there are human preferences (Paul and Elder, 1996).

Other ways to classify questions use a variety of labels: hypothetical, lower-and-higher-level, factual, abstract, convergent, divergent, focused, conceptual, philosophical, dichotomous, analytical, strategic, operational, and so on.

> We are in the age of "search-culture," in which Google and other search engines are leading us into a future rich with an abundance of correct answers along with an accompanying naïve sense of certainty. In the future, we will be able to answer the question, but will we be bright enough to ask it?
>
> —*Brockman, 2005*

Rather than depending on any single question taxonomy for all situations, facilitators base their questioning on the type of process framework required to achieve a group's objectives. Once you have decided on a process framework, you develop questions on the basis of key points in the framework, your intentions, the purpose of the session, expected outcomes, and how much time you want to spend.

If you are opening an in-house, half-day workshop for six people who have been working together for a year and are going to start a new project, then refer to the process framework in Chapter Four to create a new question for this situation. Two useful ones might be, "What is one thing you have learned as a result of being a member of this team?" and "What is one thing you would like to learn by working on this new initiative?"

Planned Questioning

Whether facilitating an in-house meeting, a national workshop, a regional think tank, or a global issues forum, facilitators usually prepare some of their questions well in advance as part of a workshop design or script. They also create some questions on the spot in response to what is going on in a session.

Given the evolving nature of process, sometimes questions that are planned in advance may end up tweaked, dropped, or moved to another place according to the facilitator's assessment of the situation. Questions in a more formal agenda are less likely to be changed on the spot.

It is the process framework that guides the facilitator in making planned, conscious decisions—both before and during a process—about which questions to use and when. If you find that a question isn't working particularly well, you can lean on your process framework to consider what other options might be more appropriate.

Closed and Open Questions

Facilitators use two general question types: closed and open. Each produces its own type of answer and has specific benefits and drawbacks in terms of group process.

Closed Questions
Closed questions require simple, specific answers and are most appropriate in a situation where one answer is preferred over another (yes or no, right or wrong, more or less). Closed questions also elicit unequivocal and often quantitative

responses. For example, "How many people are on this team?" "When was this policy initially drafted?" "Whom do you call if you need support?" "How many people are needed on this committee to ensure that it is effective and efficient?"

You can also use closed questions to get specific information from a participant, or as a part of issues analysis, problem solving, or enabling action: "If you decide to take this route, what is the first step, from a legal perspective?"

Closed questions are helpful when you want detailed feedback about a situation ("Who supports this policy?") or when you want participants to edit something written, such as a mission statement or a list of values. Closed questions also work when group members are prioritizing a list, as in selecting key directions in strategic planning.

Closed questions have disadvantages in certain situations (Gazda and others, 1984). If you are trying to encourage group members to open up or give a detailed response, closed questions that elicit a brief factual response may discourage candor and shut down conversation.

Facilitators often want to motivate participants to ask their own questions, both of themselves and of one another. Too many closed questions can discourage participants from reflecting on the situation or developing a solution in collaboration with other group members.

Closed questions may also encourage participants to become dependent on a facilitator for asking leading questions that steer participants to a supposed right answer. In this situation, group members start to expect more from the facilitator and less from themselves; the facilitator has then abdicated her primarily content-neutral position (see discussion of integrity in Chapter Two) and has become a problem solver or content expert.

Similarly, a facilitator may ask questions in such a way that the group "discovers" a conclusion already held by the facilitator. This Socratic approach, though appropriate in some learning situations, is inappropriate for a content-neutral facilitator.

Situations are not always black and white. We often facilitate in areas where, because of our experience in a particular field, we know as much about the content as participants do. In such a situation, it is important to ask questions and offer content in a way that encourages participants to think and decide for themselves. Dependency inhibits group maturation because members do not develop confidence in their ability to solve their own problems.

1

Open Questions

Open questions can't be answered simply. They require some thought, often include choices, and result in a developed answer. Two examples: "What factors contributed to your success this year?" "Where do you see the current reorganization taking the company?"

Open questions work well when you are trying to stimulate discussion and encourage critical reflection ("What approaches have you taken in the past year? How did they work out?") or want a group to engage in discussion leading to consensus ("What are the supports and barriers in this situation? What are the production implications of these supports and barriers?").

Open questions invite people to explore their thoughts, feelings, and perspectives on a subject:

How do you feel when you can't get to see your boss?

How do you think we can get employees to take more responsibility for getting things done?

How do you think we should address this problem?

What would you do if . . . ?

You can also use open questions effectively when you think a group has reached a decision prematurely and needs to explore additional dimensions of an issue ("I'm wondering if this decision might be a little premature. Are there other issues mentioned in the research report that need consideration?"). On the other hand, if you are coming to the end of a decision-making process and there seems to be implicit agreement on a conclusion, an open question can cause participants to needlessly reexamine an existing but unstated consensus. Check your inference about a possible agreement and if you are correct, move on.

There are disadvantages to using open questions. If you have a limited amount of time for introductions, asking an open question extends your timeline and frustrates participants who are anxious to get into content. Participants may grow uneasy if you ask an open question that encourages discussion but you have only five minutes left to wrap up a session. They may find it frustrating to be invited to participate in a stimulating interchange that requires them to abandon their agenda timeline.

SKILLS FOR CONSCIOUS QUESTIONING

1

Eight guiding principles and related skills support facilitators in creating and asking questions that work hard for a group (Figure 1.4).

Customize for Context

There is no best way to facilitate, no standardized model or approach that works in all (or even most) situations. Each group is unique and requires a customized approach for addressing specific challenges. This uniqueness creates an intriguing and complex dynamic for facilitators.

Context is the situation and the circumstances that weave together to frame a group's experience. Context comprises a variety of factors, among them the purpose and objectives of a process; the literacy level of participants; the resources available for next steps; and the nature, length, and commitment of the sponsoring organization. Context also includes the history of the group, how members have worked together in the past, and their interpersonal dynamics, motives, personalities, learning styles, body language, decision-making preferences, power bases, political orientation, cultural heritage, academic background, and familial

Guiding Principles

1. Customize for context.

2. Create inviting questions.

3. Clarify assumptions.

4. Ask with sensitivity.

5. Pay attention to risk and anxiety.

6. Maintain a participant-observer stance.

7. Consider "why?" carefully.

8. If in doubt, check it out.

Figure 1.4. Guiding Principles.

1

Questions can be like coins tinkling in our pockets. They have their own currency and we can never be quite sure how far our money will get us. Some are needed for purchasing immediate clarity; others are more suited for long-term investment; a few should be buried in the ground and dug up only on rainy days.

—*Moclair, 2002*

history. It also involves participants' work and life experiences. Add to these dynamics the facilitator's own style, approach, background, body language, and experience, and you have a complex mix!

Questions that work well in one context may be completely inappropriate in another. You can successfully ask a group of senior managers what leadership skills they think are required to function well in their industry, but the same question is not likely to be as effective with inexperienced managers. A group of recreation leaders are more likely to respond well to an introductory question that has a "fun" orientation than are a group of stressed-out, time-pressed lawyers focused on task and efficiency.

Pay attention to nuance in questions. A slight or subtle variation in use of words can fine-tune a question so that it delivers exactly what is needed to support group members in achieving outcomes; by changing one word (as in replacing *why* with *what* or *how*) you can completely alter the tone of a question.

Use this checklist to think about nuance in your questions:

• What is the context for this group?

• What are the objectives and expected outcomes for this process? How do they fit with the organization's mission, values, and strategic directions?

• What makes this group unique (experience, cultural diversity, gender)?

> Prompt: How can the uniqueness of this group be embedded in the questions we ask? (See Chapter Three for information on prompts.)

• Given the experience and expertise of group members, what are they likely to be most comfortable discussing? least comfortable?

> Tip: Be sure to check out inferences like this one (about comfort level) with group members.

• Is this question appropriate to how long the group has been working together and their stage of development?

Create Inviting Questions

Not all questions invite a response. Some may discourage a response, as through the use of inappropriate humor, sarcasm, or a condescending put-down. Ending a question with "Don't you agree?" or "Haven't you experienced this?" conveys too much authority to tempt a timid respondent to reply with anything but a positive response. Similarly, a question that begins with "You mean you haven't heard of . . . ?" does not invite disclosure.

There is a price for asking questions poorly. Participants who feel uncomfortable or alienated by the questions you ask are likely to become disengaged and lose ownership for the process. Here are tips on how to create inviting questions that encourage participants to respond.

• Ensure that questions are *relevant* (related to your overall purpose and specific objectives), *challenging* (stimulating people to think), and *honest* (not involving a trick or deception).

• Don't ask leading questions. The answer to a question should not be in the question; it should be in the participant.

• If you already know, don't ask the question; just offer the answer. Facilitation is not teaching. Good discussion seeks a way for people to explore ideas. Adults participating in a group discussion or decision-making process do not usually need to be tested on facts. Sometimes, if participants seem hesitant about responding to a question, I say, "When I ask a question I'm not looking for a 'right' or predetermined answer. I want to know what you think. This is not a test; it's a discussion."

• Avoid "asking down." Sometimes a facilitator needs to define or explain a word or phrase in a question, but if done incorrectly it can be perceived as condescending. Here is a question that talks down to participants: "How do you feel about your income tax—that is, the amount you have to pay the government on the money you take in during the year?" By inverting the term and the explanation, the question is much less condescending: "How do you feel about the amount you have to pay the government on the money you take in during the year—that is, your income tax?" (Payne, 1951, p. 116). Giving the explanation first and the definition second is a more conversational approach and avoids asking down.

• Choose words carefully. Use words that all the respondents will understand, avoiding special terminology, acronyms, and words with more than one meaning (*any* may mean "every," "some," or "only one"; *see* may mean "observe" or "visit a doctor or lawyer" (Payne, quoted in Sudman and Bradburn, 1982, p. 49).

• Clear questions invite answers; questions with more than one interpretation usually invite anxiety. If you ask, "Have you ever used simultaneous translation?" participants may be reluctant to respond because they may not know whether you are talking about whisper translators or the entire technology of live translation with microphones on tables and participant receivers for various languages. If you ask, "Have you used individual receivers and microphones on tables for simultaneous translation?" participants understand exactly what you mean; they hear the explanation first and the terminology second and are more likely to respond confidently.

• Take time to think through each question before asking it. Rephrasing a question several times confuses the listener and discourages a response.

• Keep questions simple. This doesn't mean easy or simplistic. "Envision a situation three years from now when our production problems have been addressed, people are happy at work, customers are satisfied, and market share is up. What do we need to do first to make this a reality?" This question is unfocused, long, and confusing. Instead, begin with a simple, single part of the question: "Imagine that it is three years from today and our production problems have been addressed. What do you see going on that is different from today?" If the group is large enough, split the question into four sections and have one quarter of the group answer one part of the question while other quarters are doing other parts.

• No one likes to appear foolish or ignorant. Avoid asking questions that cause people to lose face in a group. To reduce the threat in a challenging question, use an opening phrase such as, "Has anyone come across . . . ?" or "Have you ever run into . . . ?" or "Does anyone recall . . . ?" or "Has anyone had any experience with . . . ?"

• Not all questions need to be answered publicly. Sometimes a "to think about" question at the end of the day is designed to encourage critical reflection not meant for sharing with anyone. You may ask a question to launch an important discussion that results in dialogue over lunch and stays within the confines of three or four people's experience: "Take some time over lunch to reflect on how much energy you want to commit to this initiative, given your personal situation. Your conclusions will be helpful in preparing you to discuss the extent to which you want to be engaged in the next steps." Questions like this one are designed to support interaction and shared perspectives; the responses don't always need to be reported back in plenary.

• Read and respond to the nonverbal messages or "vibes" in a group while you are asking a question. You may want to comment on what you are noticing. People can make it obvious through their body language that they think a question is inappropriate; you can then respond, "Looks like this question may be problematic. Can you help me understand what's not working here?"

Clarify Assumptions

Most questions have assumptions in them that influence their meaning, impact, and effectiveness.

The question "How can we improve our sales record over the next six months?" makes several assumptions: that "we" have the power and commitment to improve, that the sales record needs to be improved, that a significant change can happen in six months, that the record is not up to par. If you check assumptions before asking a question of this sort, you can save a lot of time discussing options for action that cannot be implemented.

Prior to using a key question that does not seem right, consult with others who have a stake in the outcome to get their opinion on the question and clarify possible assumptions. Probing for assumptions sends the message, "We need to listen to each other carefully in order to identify and understand what each of us is assuming. Misunderstandings can lead to poor outcomes for all of us."

Facilitators need to check on assumptions in both the questions they ask and those asked by others:

Am I correct in thinking that there is an assumption about . . . in your
     question?

Do you think this assumption is true for our competitors?

Does this question stand on its own, or do we need to ask other questions first?

How long has that assumption been around?

How many here agree with this assumption?

I was assuming that . . . and it sounds as if you are making a slightly different assumption. Is this correct?

Is this assumption likely to be valid six months from now?

Our approach to this problem depends on the assumption that. . . . Is this assumption true for everyone here?

Your question sounds like a statement to me. Are you assuming that . . . ?

This is what I'm assuming: . . . Is that what you were assuming?

What assumption is this based on?

Would . . . (a person or group with another perspective) make a different assumption from the one in this question?

An additional benefit of checking assumptions may be to discover that the initial question was really several smaller ones that are part of getting to a discussion about what needs to happen next. Thus examining the question closely for assumptions contributes to better understanding of the overall process.

Ask with Sensitivity

Because a question can evoke a strong emotional reaction, it is important to be sensitive to how and when you ask it (tone, voice level, timing, speed of delivery, facial expression, bodily stance, eye contact). You may pose questions on an emotional spectrum that ranges from distant (even hostile) formality to warm geniality. "What do you think?" can communicate many meanings, depending on the questioner's inflection, emphasis, and demeanor (Christensen, Gavin, and Sweet, 1991).

Here are some suggestions for enhancing your sensitivity in asking questions.

• Be aware of your body language in asking questions. Are your physical posture, eye contact, and tone of voice supportive and engaging? Or, by contrast, (1) are you physically towering over a group of people who are feeling intimidated? (2) Do you cross your arms over your chest when you think a question is going to be resisted? (3) Do you ask questions while writing on a flipchart with your back to the group? (4) Whom do you have eye contact with when you ask a question of an entire group? (5) Does your tone of voice sound as if you are commanding rather than inquiring?

• Use a bridge or linking sentence to introduce a sensitive question. For example, "Everyone in this room has been rejected on a promising cold call. Think about the last time this happened to you. What was your initial reaction when you realized you were going to be turned down?"

• Ask permission to pose a question that is particularly sensitive: "May I ask how you decided to do it this way?" or "May I ask you a couple of questions about the situation in your office?"

• When a question is too intrusive participants could feel taken by surprise and be unable to respond. Not everyone has the presence of mind to say, "I find that question intrusive and am not prepared to respond right now." By reviewing your questions and approach with your client or planning committee, you can explore what question types or topics might be considered too intrusive for group members.

• Use self-disclosure to express sensitivity. For example, "One of the things I've learned over the past two years as president of this board is the importance of sticking to policy decisions and staying out of operations. Where do you think this particular agenda item belongs: in policy or operations?"

• Use humor carefully. Generally speaking, if people laugh at the expense of others then the humor is not appropriate. Be particularly careful about sensitive topics and issues in politically correct areas—for instance, "-isms" such as racism and sexism.

1

Accommodate Risk and Anxiety

Questions vary as to the risk and anxiety they convey in a specific situation. Sometimes questions need to be low in risk, easygoing, and relatively free of tension. At other times—for example, when a group needs to explore difficult issues—questions will carry a higher level of risk and anxiety.

Generally speaking, the level of risk or anxiety goes up when group members feel that a question is very difficult, or there is a lot at stake in the answer, or there is a right answer and they don't know what it is, or the potential level of confrontation or disclosure in a response makes participants feel uncomfortable.

Here are some suggestions that help facilitators attend to the risk factor in questioning.

• Normalize difficult questions and responses. If a regional manager is facilitating planning with a group of account managers who have not met quota, the question, "What prevented you from reaching quota this quarter?" can be risky, particularly if the regional manager is part of the discussion. Normalizing the challenges that account managers have faced can help reduce the risk in responding. For example, the regional manager (in a facilitating role) could say, "Every one of us has felt the impact of company policy changes in our accounts this quarter, but we haven't given up, and that's a good thing. We can learn a lot about what we've been through and how we might act in a similar situation by sharing our perspectives on this. So let's open up and talk candidly: What prevented us from reaching quota this quarter? I'll start off with something I think I could have managed better." Understanding and paying attention to the context for a process helps determine the level of risk in a question. In this example, the context makes it clear that the question is best asked by the regional manager, who is also a participant in the group.

> When facilitating social change initiatives, strategic questions can be used to get ideas and potential solutions to emerge from the people affected; create a neutral and common ground for collaborative effort; create respect and value for the experience of others; listen to people's pain; ask the "unaskable"; create options; dig deeper; support empowerment.
>
> —*Peavey, 1994 (adapted)*

20

1

• Before asking questions, be clear with group members about what is confidential (see the discussion of clarifying confidentiality in Chapter Two) and who will be informed about what was said or decided.

• Start with low-risk questions that involve minimal challenge and require little self-disclosure before moving to higher-risk questions. Similarly, begin with questions that people are no doubt able to answer (recounting an event, or a personal opinion on background materials) so that you can build on their success before moving on to more difficult questions related to personal views on a controversial topic.

• Prepare participants for "big questions." They go by a number of names: strategic, audacious, powerful, great, meaningful. They are also usually focused on facilitating some form of significant change: personal, team, organizational, social, ecological, political, governmental. As such, there is usually a fairly high level of risk and anxiety involved.

• Give participants a few minutes to review their background materials before answering: "Review the premeeting paper and then jot down all the ideas that come to mind to describe your options for action." Then ask them to share their ideas with a partner and develop a list of three or four priorities. These two tasks help people bridge into an answer.

• When appropriate, create an opportunity for people to respond anonymously to questions (through card sorting, multivoting, sealed envelopes, interviews, or the Internet). Big questions require courage, determination, and a fairly high level of comfort with risk, both to ask and to answer. They must also be asked by a facilitator who knows himself, the group, and the situation well in order to be successful.

> The 2005 Edge Question has generated many eye-opening responses from a "who's who" of third culture scientists and science-minded thinkers: "Great minds can sometimes guess the truth before they have either the evidence or arguments for it. What do you believe is true even though you cannot prove it?"
>
> —Brockman, 2005

A general rule of thumb for big questions is that there should be no surprises. If you know you have a tough question coming up, offer some preparation time so that group members can think about what they want to say. Here are some options for preparing participants for big questions.

• Make questions available in the premeeting package—for example, "During the first part of the session we will be asking you to respond to three questions. Please come prepared with a brief response to each one. (1) When you think about our Employee Assistance Programs in terms of the next two years, what do you think our biggest challenge or problem is going to be? (2) What are we doing now with respect to our human resources challenge that is *not* going to be helpful in the future? (3) What are we doing now with respect to our human resources challenge that is going to be helpful in the future?"

• Plan the introduction of a big question such that people have time to consider it before answering. Consider an example from a one-day planning session. Before the morning break, we stated: "After the break we will be listening to a presentation by Dr. Doestoomuch. He will speak for an hour before lunch, and then there will be a question-and-answer period after lunch. While you are listening to him, please take notes on how to do more with less—a question that we will be discussing after lunch." Before lunch, the group was again reminded of the question: "As I mentioned earlier, we will be discussing the question of how to do more with less after lunch. You may want to keep this in the back of your mind over lunch—or even discuss it while you are enjoying the flaming baked Alaska."

Maintain a Participant-Observer Stance

A facilitator who is in a participant-observer stance is present to what group members are working on (content) while also noticing and intervening to support group development (process) and progress toward outcomes (process framework). This dual role with respect to content and process includes noticing how questions are working in the context of a process framework and making decisions related to follow-up queries.

• Enable all perspectives to be heard on an issue. Intervene to ensure that all participants have an opportunity to share ideas and concerns in response to questions ("Are there any perspectives that we haven't heard?" "Who has a different take on this issue?").

> Tip: Summarize the perspectives you have heard so far and then ask for any additional views.

• Keep your process framework in mind so that you are clear about where you are, where you have been, and where you want to go next.

• The right questions enable people to talk about what is important to them, thus building ownership and motivation for addressing issues. Monitor the amount of air time (talking time) on an issue and who is doing the talking: the more air time people have, the more likely they are to take ownership for addressing a challenge. Ownership that is well developed during a workshop can extend into knowledge translation (closing the gap between what we know and what we do) and follow-up action long after a workshop is over.

• Leverage the potential power of positive politics (Strachan, Shaw, Kent, and Tomlinson, 1986). Although the word *politics* often conjures up images of frustration, manipulation, and self-interest, "positive politics" involves all the activities that people engage in to gain support for their ideas and includes persuasive discussion, marshalling support, forming coalitions, and other activities. Political processes are a normal and predictable part of both workshops and organizational life and, if carried on in a positive manner, can contribute significantly to the vitality of processes by fostering an opportunity for people to clarify their ideas, engage in constructive discussion, and help determine the path their organization takes. Here are examples of questions to leverage positive politics:

Does anyone think that their case has not been presented comprehensively?

Is there any important information that some people in this discussion might have that others might not have?

Let's make sure that we aren't overstating or understating the challenges in this issue. Do you think we have a balanced perspective here, before we move on?

Sounds like there is a lot of interest in this particular point of view. Who would like to take this discussion further over lunch?

We've said that we want to take an inclusive approach to this challenge. Can you think of any key stakeholder groups who should be involved in this process that we haven't engaged to date?

1

Consider "Why?" Carefully

Although "Why?" can be used effectively in (or as) an open question, it can also give the impression of an aggressive interrogation ("Why didn't you try the solution we suggested?"). The inference is that the respondent has failed or done something wrong.

You can avoid the potential defensiveness that is likely with *why* by substituting *how, what,* or *when* (for example, "What made you decide to take a different tack on this?").

Don't ask *why* when feelings run high (Tomlinson and Strachan, 1996). When you ask "Why?" in an emotional situation, people often feel accused or blamed, which tends to initiate a defensive reaction. In an emotional situation, it is often difficult for people to state why they did something or justify an action. They may be able to explain how something happened or what they did, but if they feel backed into a corner by a demand for a reason then they may become intimidated and just say the first thing that comes to mind, or make something up to rationalize the situation.

• Asking why may also serve to take the experience away from the individual and transfer it to an authority figure—you, as facilitator. Facilitators who ask for an *explanation* ("How did that happen?" or "What did you think about that?") are more likely to get accurate and truthful responses in a difficult situation than those who ask for a *reason*. In an emotional situation, you can avoid intimidating participants and enable them to give a more thoughtful answer if you "bye the why."

• Five whys: one questioning technique that can be effective for getting to the root cause of a problem is to ask a series of five "Why . . ." questions, each building on the previous response.

Used tactfully and without blame to solve a problem, this technique works well. However, in a tense environment where the answer to these questions could end in potential legal liability, loss of face, a charge of incompetence, or possible job loss, the process could be disastrous and must be handled carefully.

When in Doubt, Check It Out

If you are not sure you have the right question to support a process, consult with others as to whether the question makes sense to them. Trust your feeling of uneasiness about a question: it is likely based on experience.

Here are some questions you can ask others if you are in doubt about the appropriateness of a question. As with other lists in this book, choose the ones that work for your situation; not all questions apply to all situations.

Are there aspects of this question that are unclear? If so, how can we clarify?

Could this question be misinterpreted by various stakeholders? If so, how could we clear that up?

Does the answer to this question depend on other questions that must be answered first? If so, where should we position this question?

Does the question acknowledge the larger context in which it is being asked [regarding interrelated factors, or a systems response]?

Does the question have a clear focus that is directed toward the outcomes of the process?

Does the question have the right amount of tension to entice good thinking?

Does the question help participants make sense of the area under discussion?

Does the question lead participants toward an answer? [If so, delete any unnecessary information and ask the question objectively.]

Does the question relate to what is unique about the topic being discussed?

Does this question have the potential to initiate a breakthrough discussion with respect to projected outcomes?

Will the response to this question make a difference in terms of our objectives?

How much difficulty will people have in answering this question?

In what ways might people answer this question in this group? (*Variation:* Substitute "interpret" for *answer.*)

1

Will participants feel comfortable saying "I don't know" in response to this question?

Is the question at the right level for the group you are working with?

Is the question simple?

> **Tip: Simple doesn't mean easy or simplistic.**

Is there anything about this question that could disrupt the flow of our agenda?

Is there more than one query in the question? If so, separate each one into its own question.

We have a number of . . . in this group. Would they interpret this question differently than other participants, such as . . . ?

What are the assumptions in this question?

> Prompt: Do they fit the content and context of our group?

Why should we ask this question?

Will this question help people help themselves with respect to the issue being discussed?

REMINDERS

Asking questions is a skill acquired over time and with experience. While we are acquiring experience, we often pick up habits, not all of which are helpful. Table 1.1 presents some tips as basic reminders for facilitators (Hunsaker and Alessandra, 1980; Strachan, 1988).

Instead of Asking . . .	Try Asking . . .	So That . . .
Do you understand the question? (or) Do you understand the task? (or) Who doesn't understand this?	Did I explain the task clearly?	The responsibility for making the question or the task clear remains with the facilitator, not with the participant.
Who is responsible for supplying the flip charts?	Where can we get more flip chart paper?	The focus is on correcting the problem rather than placing blame.
Why are you feeling so upset?	How did the situation get to this point?	The question invites a response rather than discouraging one.
What are your options for ensuring that you are successful?	Let's brainstorm some options for addressing this problem. Be creative—in brainstorming there are no wrong answers.	The respondent is not made to feel defensive about answering the question; the respondent doesn't feel that she has to come up with all the right possibilities.
We're almost finished, don't you think?	What's your sense of where we are in terms of the whole project?	You are not requesting agreement. The authority implicit in "Don't you think?" implies that any disagreement must be mistaken—hardly a message to stimulate free inquiry (Christensen, Gavin, and Sweet, 1991).

Figure 1.5. Reminders.   *(continued)*

1

Instead of Asking . . .	Try Asking . . .	So That . . .
Why did you stop there instead of finishing the task?	What was happening for you when you stopped there?	The respondent does not feel pressured to develop a reason; instead she can simply describe what is happening for her.
What sort of data do you have to back up your opinion?	Tell me more. Has anyone researched this?	You are not putting the respondent in a defensive, weaker position.
Are things still pretty awful with your new supervisor?	How are things going now with your new supervisor?	You avoid assuming a negative response; you offer the opportunity for a constructive response.
Let me be the devil's advocate. How can we avoid taking this route to solve this problem?	What other ways can you think of to solve this problem? (or) What about the point of view that . . . ? (or) What are all our options here?	An opposing view is not perceived to be negative (as in belonging to the devil); group members don't lose sight of who believes what and what has already been said.
Why did your team get such a bad review on that project?	What were the key factors that influenced how that project turned out?	You invite an honest, reflective response rather than a defensive rationalization.
Define the word *strategic* for the purposes of this discussion.	How are you using the word *strategic* in this discussion?	The respondent feels less pressure to respond with a supposed right answer; asking for a description instead of a definition gives more permission to extend an individual perspective.

Figure 1.5. Reminders. *(continued)*

1

Instead of Asking . . .	Try Asking . . .	So That . . .
Do you agree or disagree?	What does that sound like to you? (or) Does this seem like a sensible approach? (or) How important is this issue to you? (or) Would you use this approach in your department?	You avoid forcing the respondent into an either-or answer; you can find out where respondents stand on a topic.
Do you think that having lobbyists in your planning session will taint the agreement-building process?	Who has had experience facilitating lobbyists? How did the decision-making process go? (Prompt: Did their involvement affect how decisions were made?)	You encourage a variety of opinions; you avoid asking questions that lead participants to a desired answer.
How might this change in the foreseeable future?	Given your human resources situation, how might this situation change over the next six months?	You are specific when referring to a situation and a time period.
What are the big conflicts we are facing now in our team?	One of the characteristics of a well-functioning team is conflict. Today I want to discuss how we are successful in dealing with conflict among ourselves and where our challenges are. So let's begin. From your perspective, what is one area where we are dealing well with conflict?	You build a bridge or linking sentence when introducing sensitive questions; participants feel support for being candid; you normalize what people are experiencing (they realize that their responses are not unusual).

Figure 1.5. Reminders. *(continued)*

Instead of Asking . . .	Try Asking . . .	So That . . .
Which of these objectives is the most important?	What is one question you want answered by the end of this session?	The focus of the question is clearly on participants' specific learning needs; you acknowledge participants' questions as important.
She did a really good job on that one, don't you think?	Did her work meet your expectations?	You avoid a persuasive tag at the end of the question; a tag can signal a statement disguised as a question.

Figure 1.5. Reminders. *(continued)*

2 Core Facilitation Values

Values are the deeply held beliefs about what is right that guide behavior. Core facilitation values are statements of ideals that are made operational through conscious effort over many years.

When I first started to facilitate professionally, I knew that it was important to be as objective as possible and that respect for participants was essential. I also knew that the more I could relax and be myself in working with groups, the better I felt about the whole process as well as the final product. However, it was not until I had spent time clarifying values with clients that I truly felt the need to be clear about my own core facilitation values.

Several facilitators have commented on the importance of core values. Chris Argyris has written about the values of "valid information, free and informed choice and internal commitment to the choice" (Argyris, 1970). Roger Schwarz, Anne Davidson, and others added a fourth value of compassion to these three (Schwarz, Davidson, Carlson, and McKinney, 2005). John Heron talks about the need to respect "the autonomy and wholeness" of the learner (1993, p. 16). Others emphasize core values in group decision-making processes, such as full participation, mutual understanding, inclusive solutions, and shared responsibility (Kaner and others, 1996). The core values espoused by the International Association of Facilitators are inclusiveness, global scope, participation, celebration, innovative form, and social responsibility (http://www.iaf-world.org, March, 2006).

In our practice, three core values anchor how we behave as facilitators and in particular how we ask questions: integrity, authenticity, and mutual respect. Integrity reflects professional honesty, fairness, and objectivity, all of which serve

2

to honor the process we are facilitating. Authenticity is about being genuine—being sincere and caring with yourself and others. Mutual respect is about making the effort to understand people, honoring their rights and perspectives.

The facilitator's role is to model these values and enable their implementation while working with group members. Figure 2.1 suggests key behaviors to guide facilitators when acting on these three values.

VALUES INTO ACTION

Asking questions effectively is both a science and an art. The science part happens through research focused on skill development in such disciplines as psychology, organization development, sociology, group process, and facilitation. The art comes in when the facilitator appreciates the context in which questions are being asked and acts on her values along with the synergy of her experience and her intuition to guide questioning.

1. Integrity	2. Authenticity	3. Mutual Respect
a. Maintain objectivity	a. Build group ownership for outcomes	a. Enable equity
b. Clarify confidentiality	b. Minimize self-deception	b. Clarify group norms
c. Be sensitive to conflicts of interest	c. Be clear about intentions	c. Respect exchange times
d. Avoid collusion	d. Acknowledge problems	d. Encourage direct interaction
e. Ask questions fairly	e. Be honest	e. Be patient; whose silence is it?
f. Determine authorship	f. Be present; tune in	f. Respect the energy in the group
g. Address imbalances in power and information	g. Hear your client's perspective	

Figure 2.1. Core Facilitation Values.

The final goal for facilitators is theory and values into action—science and art combined in effective practice. When this is in place, you are so comfortable with both the art and the science that they are one in how you act.

INTEGRITY

Integrity is about professional honesty (not tactless aggression), objectivity, and freedom from conflict of interest. Working with others in groups is often complex, confusing, and challenging; it is not always easy to maintain professional integrity while facilitating complex processes.

In asking and answering questions, facilitators are responsible for their own professional integrity as well as for the integrity of the process being used to achieve objectives. Seven specific aspects of integrity in questioning are seen in Figure 2.2.

Guidelines for Asking Questions with Integrity

Here are suggestions to help facilitators translate the value of integrity into action when asking questions.

Content neutrality means not taking a position on the issues at hand; not having a position or a stake in the outcome. Process neutrality means not advocating for certain kinds of processes such as brainstorming. We found the power in the role of the facilitator was in becoming content-neutral and a process advocate.

—Kaner and others, 1996

Maintain Objectivity

Being objective is the heart of facilitators' integrity and the basis of their contracts with clients. Although a distinction can be made between objectivity and *neutrality* in talking about the facilitator's role, in this book the words are used interchangeably to emphasize the facilitator's disinterested nature with respect to content-based decision making. The objective or neutral facilitator is impartial, fair, and unbiased with respect to the content being discussed. She may have an opinion on the content, but she does not let that personal bias unduly influence group decision making.

1. Integrity	2. Authenticity	3. Mutual Respect
a. Maintain objectivity	a. Build group ownership for outcomes	a. Enable equity
b. Clarify confidentiality	b. Minimize self-deception	b. Clarify group norms
c. Be sensitive to conflicts of interest	c. Be clear about intentions	c. Respect exchange times
d. Avoid collusion	d. Acknowledge problems	d. Encourage direct interaction
e. Ask questions fairly	e. Be honest	e. Be patient; whose silence is it?
f. Determine authorship	f. Be present; tune in	f. Respect the energy in the group
g. Address imbalances in power and information	g. Hear your client's perspective	

Figure 2.2. Core Facilitation Values: Integrity.

One of the strongest skills in a facilitator's toolkit is being able to *maintain a participant-observer stance.* This skill enables a facilitator to observe what is happening, notice group dynamics, track the development of content, and acknowledge her personal opinion while staying firmly grounded in the contract with the client and the group. This skill can be particularly valuable in a challenging situation where she needs heightened consciousness about questions in a process, as in clarifying critical feedback or managing conflict.

Confirm the roles of chair and/or facilitator. I am occasionally asked (as an external person) to facilitate a meeting along with a chairperson. This can happen for a number of reasons. A not-for-profit organization might want to provide some profile to a volunteer chair during a session, a committee chair might have special content expertise in an area, or a client might have some training or expertise in facilitation and want to put it to use.

Cofacilitating with someone who has an interest in the outcome of a session may result in a conflict of interest that puts your integrity as a facilitator at stake. In legal terms, the interested person is said to have a "reasonable expectation of bias." Questions of *what, when, why,* and *how* can have a significant impact on what, when, why, and how decisions are made.

It is important to clarify and confirm your role as facilitator, as well as the role of the chairperson. We usually have the chairperson introduce the meeting, give a brief history of what led up to the session, describe the motivation for calling people together, and explain why there is an external facilitator. Then the chairperson formally hands the meeting over to the facilitator so that there is no confusion about who is managing the process. At this point, two things happen: the chairperson becomes a full participant along with others involved in the session, and we confirm that the facilitator is to be content-neutral and an advocate for a healthy and productive process.

Clarify Confidentiality

Confidentiality can be an important part of integrity in facilitation. Be clear about what aspects of confidentiality can and cannot be negotiated. Confidentiality and nondisclosure clauses in a contract are a common safeguard for clients who are concerned about sensitive subjects such as job security, privacy legislation to guard personal information, corporate espionage, or confidential policies.

Norms for confidentiality in group processes vary with the client and need to be confirmed on the basis of the purpose and objectives of a process. Confidentiality can be about what is communicated by participants during a session in response to such questions as "Can personal examples be used?" and "What topics are on or off the table?" It can also be about what people say after a session ("What can be communicated about what was discussed or took place during this session?" "What is and is not in the public domain?").

Here are sample questions to initiate discussion about confidentiality in a group:

Are there aspects of this initiative that are confidential or nonnegotiable when it comes to discussion?

There are three media representatives included on your invitation list. We have three speakers who will be talking about their personal experiences with

35

mental illness. Will they speak candidly about their experiences if they know the media will be present? (Or: Given the stigma attached to mental illness, has anyone contacted them to see whether they are comfortable with this situation?)

This forum will engage the presidents of both unions and private sector corporations on some long-standing contentious topics. Are there confidentiality issues that we need to discuss such as what is on or off the table at this event?

This public forum on enhancing national security is designed to be as open as possible. Can we agree ahead of time on any topics that are not open for discussion?

Prompts: How might this have an impact on the questions we ask?

Be clear and specific about norms for confidentiality in a session, as in these examples:

Be candid and direct in your questions. We need open and thoughtful critical reflection to make this process work. No names will be attached to specific comments in the report.

Please be both open and caring with feedback. Our report will disclose only key decisions, not discussion leading up to decisions. Discussion will remain confidential to members of this group.

This meeting is off the record. We agree that there will be no report and that none of the parties involved will discuss any aspect of the meeting with others.

When asking questions of others, avoid confidential topics such as. . . .

Be Sensitive to Conflicts of Interest

A facilitator is in a conflict of interest when her interests, affiliations, or obligations interfere with her position of trust with a group, which requires her to exercise her judgment in support of group process. All actual and potential conflicts of interest must be declared by facilitators and discussed with appropriate individuals to confirm how to proceed.

If you are in a conflict of interest, you jeopardize the integrity of your role as an objective facilitator. Here are six common examples of potential conflict of interest where how, when, and why you ask questions could interfere with your position of trust as a facilitator.

Marketing on your client's nickel. Have you ever been in a training or planning session where you thought the examples offered by the facilitator had more to do with his telling you about his company's recent successes than about the issue being discussed? If the answer to the question, "What's really going on here?" is that the facilitator is too focused on building his consulting practice or on selling publications, then both the facilitator and the process lack authenticity. Facilitators can attend to this potential conflict of interest by continuously reflecting on linking what they say, the stories they tell, and who stands to benefit from these interventions.

Access to power and influence. Facilitators can be seen as an asset to the board of directors thanks to the skill set they can bring to the table. If you are asked to join a board in a content area in which you work and where you stand to benefit, it is important to ask yourself whether accepting the position would result in your:

- Being perceived to be in the pocket of the organization and therefore promoting its perspective and objectives when facilitating

- Having inappropriate access to inside information that would taint your objectivity when working in that field

- Having unfair access to positional power and authority that other facilitators (competitors) would not have, that is, your private interests benefit from your public service

The individual and the group. If your client is thinking about hiring or promoting someone who is a participant in a session and asks you to offer some observations on the person, you cannot take on that role and still maintain the neutrality participants are counting on.

If you accede to the client's request, you are in conflict of interest; you are facilitating the group and evaluating a participant in terms of job worthiness. For example, you may end up asking questions that test whether the group member has the knowledge required to take on the job, rather than asking questions that support a healthy process leading toward the group's objectives.

2

Several years ago in a course on negotiation offered by members of a law firm from another city, one of the facilitators said, "We are always on the look-out for new places to offer our course. Can you help us get in touch with the right people around here to see if there are any prospects?"

I felt awkward hearing this question. I wanted to learn about the topic and get value for the course fees, not be solicited for future clients. Also, some of our company's law firm clients offered similar courses, and the question therefore seemed insensitive. Hearing a sales pitch before I could even decide on the usefulness of the course meant the facilitators were in conflict of interest; they were marketing their consulting practice instead of focusing their questions on our learning objectives.

Sector interface. A common source of potential conflict of interest is when the public, nongovernmental, and private sectors interface in a facilitated process. In this situation, it is the facilitator's role to protect the integrity of the questions from conflict of interest. For example, if you found drug product advertising (private sector) in a physician education program for a society of medical specialists (nongovernmental organization) education event, you might ask, "I notice that you have included drug advertisements in the draft conference program for physician education. Does your ethics committee have a position on this?"

Issues boundaries. Sometimes you become identified with a political party, a specific perspective, or one side of a highly charged debate. It is important to clarify your boundaries as a facilitator so that you can disclose views that a client may not deem to be appropriate for his process and outcomes.

In one situation, a national religious organization with a firm and well-known view on abortion approached us to facilitate a strategic planning process for them. When we met with the president of the organization, we explained that although we felt comfortable working with them we did not share their views on abortion. The president's comment was, "I'm hiring you because I have seen your skills as process consultants and am comfortable working with you. I think the challenge here is on your side: you need to explore your heart to see if you can maintain your integrity and objectivity as process consultants while working with us. If you can, then there is no conflict of interest from my perspective. I trust you to do the best job you can." We worked with that organization for several years in a nurturing and mutually respectful relationship.

Consider a question to further clarify boundaries related to your facilitation practice: "What controversial issues, public policies, political views, or highly charged debates (if any) do you support or not support?"

Address fiduciary responsibilities. When facilitating a board or council members of an organization, it is essential to clarify their fiduciary responsibilities early in the process. Board or council members hold a position of trust with respect to others in an organization in relation to the organization's mission and goals. This trust is the defining characteristic of their fiduciary responsibilities when asking and responding to questions in a meeting, workshop, or other process.

When state or provincial representatives are asked to sit as directors on a national board, it is their fiduciary responsibility to take the perspective of a national board member, not of their provincial or state organization. This means that in responding to questions about a mission statement for the national organization their loyalties must lie in what is best for the national organization, not the potential impact on their state or provincial affiliate. The facilitator's role is to protect the integrity of the process and remind board members about their national fiduciary obligations.

Although legal action in relation to breach of fiduciary responsibility is becoming more common, many board members are unaware of this fact and how their perspective on loyalty can have a significant impact on questions and answers related to the future of the organization. If board or council members find it too difficult to harmonize their national/federal and state, provincial, or territorial foundations, they may need to review the governance of their related body to see if structures need adjustment.

Avoid Collusion

Collusion is a secret agreement, whether stated or not, with a participant, client, or cofacilitator. Collusion is inconsistent with the facilitator's role, because it requires her to withhold valid information and consequently prevents free and informed choice for certain group members. It places the interests of some group members or the client above the interests of the group as a whole (Schwarz, 1994, p. 15).

When a client requests that a facilitator ask the group a question because the client doesn't want the group to know that the question is coming from him, this is potential collusion. It is not uncommon for a group member to make a similar

2

request: "Would you ask the group if they would think about . . . ? I don't want this question to come from me."

Asking questions that are not bona fide but are meant to mollify a group can also be collusion. If you know that a client has put a topic on an agenda to avoid conflict with group members and she has no intention of taking it any further even though group members are anxious for specific action, you are colluding with the client and jeopardizing the integrity of the group process.

Integrity may be upheld by asking yourself, "Have I ever been in collusion or on the edge of colluding with a client or group member?" "What did I do?" "Would I do the same thing again?"

Ask Questions Fairly

Do you ever wonder why people tend to answer the questions that are asked in a facilitated session? Occasionally someone will say, "I'm going to pass on this one" or "I choose not to answer that question now," but this is uncommon. Most often, people answer questions simply because they are asked—as if the facilitator-participant relationship includes an obligation to respond. For this reason, a facilitator has an obligation to consider fairness when asking questions—that is, whether the questions are impartial and free from favoritism, self-interest, client-interest, bias, or deception.

Asking questions fairly is easy in a simple situation; you know what is right, you understand what you want to ask and why you want to ask it, the situation is clear, and little is at stake. However, facilitators rarely face a simple situation. What is fair is often complex and unclear, and the stakes can be very high.

Leading questions may be unethical. If your client or employer wants a specific result from a session and the group is leaning toward another conclusion, how you ask a question can prejudice the outcome. For example, if you say, "The company is losing significant revenue because of employees coming in late. What do you think we should do?" the discussion is likely to start on a very different note than if you say, "Revenues are down 7 percent this quarter. What are you noticing that could contribute to this loss?"

Preventing group decisions that differ from the client's expectations can also be unethical. On occasion, I have experienced considerable pressure from clients who want a specific outcome from a session although that outcome does not reflect the experience of participants. Acting with integrity means asking the client up front what she would do if the group wanted an outcome other than what she wants. This question can open a discussion about values and how they translate into action. As a facilitator, you need to feel comfortable using your values to support fair questioning throughout a process.

Determine Authorship

Most facilitated processes end up with various types of reports—a summary of questions and conclusions, a survey of participants, a background document, proceedings, a conference overview, a paper on a consultation. Authorship of these documents can be contentious if not settled ahead of time. This is particularly important to people in academia who receive credit for publication and may feel uncomfortable about questions related to the integrity of who gets credit for what. As soon as appropriate, ask:

- How will the work of committee members be noted?

- If an external consulting company facilitates the session and writes the report will their name be on the cover? (Or, Should the organization's name be on the cover because the consultant is in service to the organization?)

- Who will have primary and secondary authorship?

- If an internal facilitator writes the report, will he have authorship or will the team?

- Will the role of participants in this process be acknowledged in the final report?

- Will the sponsoring organization own recommendations on the basis of its copyright?

Address Imbalances in Power and Information

In most groups there is disparity in power and information among participants; this can have a significant impact on questions and responses. The power and influence of the facilitator also plays a role in what may initially seem to be subtle decisions related to group process. How we ask questions, whom we ask, how frequently we ask them, when we ask, and for what purpose—all these decisions are wrapped up in our integrity as facilitators, simply because we have power, expertise, and information that can influence the outcome of a process.

2

As facilitators, our questioning practices can ensure that difference in power and information (confidential briefings and other data) are addressed openly. Ask yourself these questions:

- Do you question people whose views are similar to yours more often than those whose views differ?

- Does everyone engaged in the process have the same background information to support discussion?

- How do you decide whom to ask or whom to call on during a session?

- Is there a pattern to who gets what questions when you are facilitating?

Several years ago, in a heated exchange during a session with faculty at a university, a participant suggested that I was reluctant to call on a particularly combative professor and that I had a responsibility to call on everyone equally. I learned a lot during that process, as well as over the ensuing years, by reflecting on the situation and whether I was acting with integrity. Can you recall a situation where you noticed a pattern in how you were asking questions?

Operationalizing the Value of Integrity

How operative is the value of integrity when you use questions in a process? Think about what you do when facilitating specific situations involving questions. In Fig-

First, ethical decisions are unavoidable in discussion settings. Precisely because a session, event or workshop mirrors the fragile personal interactions of everyday life, human relationships and the associated ethical issues are continually at stake. Second, in such settings, absolute fairness is impossible, and trade-offs and compromises are inevitable. Someone is likely to be disadvantaged or displeased by almost every action; the facilitator's only hope is to establish a rough hierarchy of values, to monitor the personal and educational impact of resulting decisions, and when in doubt, to follow that priceless maxim, "Strive to do no harm."

—*Garvin, 1991 (adapted)*

ure 2.3 we see seven behaviors related to integrity; to what extent is the value of integrity posted or operative in each of these areas of your practice?

- Posted = knowing that the value is important, talking about it, saying that you believe it is vital to effective facilitation
- Operative = acting on the value regularly, integrating it into your facilitation practice continuously

1. Integrity	Posted				Operative
a. Maintain objectivity	1	2	3	4	5
b. Clarify confidentiality	1	2	3	4	5
c. Be sensitive to conflicts of interest	1	2	3	4	5
d. Avoid collusion	1	2	3	4	5
e. Ask questions fairly	1	2	3	4	5
f. Determine authorship	1	2	3	4	5
g. Address imbalances in power and information	1	2	3	4	5

To operationalize this value further, I need to

Stop doing: _____

_____

Start doing: _____

_____

Continue doing: _____

_____

Figure 2.3. Operationalizing the Value of Integrity.

AUTHENTICITY

Authenticity is about being real and genuine. It involves avoiding self-deception and being true to yourself in working with others.

Authenticity is not acting like someone else whom you admire, or telling jokes even though that is not your style. It is the "struggle for mastery, not only of content and craft, but also of self" (Christensen et al., 1991, p. xv). It means learning to become so comfortable in your own skin that you view your knowledge and expertise as instrumental to effective group process rather than as something to be displayed.

> *There is no best personality type for facilitators. The best personality type for you is your own.*

Authenticity is a core value because it enables the facilitator to see the group more clearly, without the view being obscured by the facilitator's façade. Modeling authenticity also helps to elicit authentic responses from participants.

We have found that participants in group processes are becoming increasingly concerned about authenticity. Robert Terry identifies six factors that contribute to this preoccupation:

1. A deep and undefined sense of disconnection from the institutions and people that we believe we should be connected with

2. Information overload based on our technology-rich societies

3. An increasing mistrust of institutions, organizations, and systems

4. Development of virtual realities (for example, through technology, spin control, and disinformation)

5. An increasing fragility of a shared sense of purpose

6. The rise of relativism; that is, people feel that they can never really know what is true or real or what is good or right (adapted from Terry, 1983, pp. 114–126)

Given the presence of these factors, one constructive response a facilitator can make is to be authentic, to be genuine with participants and to ask the question

1. Integrity	2. Authenticity	3. Mutual Respect
a. Maintain objectivity	a. Build group owner- ship for outcomes	a. Enable equity
b. Clarify confidentiality	b. Minimize self- deception	b. Clarify group norms
c. Be sensitive to con- flicts of interest	c. Be clear about intentions	c. Respect exchange times
d. Avoid collusion	d. Acknowledge problems	d. Encourage direct interaction
e. Ask questions fairly	e. Be honest	e. Be patient; whose silence is it?
f. Determine authorship	f. Be present; tune in	f. Respect the energy in the group
g. Address imbalances in power and information	g. Hear your client's perspective	

Figure 2.4. Core Facilitation Values: Authenticity.

that is often uppermost in their minds—"What is really going on here?"—with skill and caring. Seven specific aspects of authenticity in questioning are shown in Figures 2.1 and 2.4.

Guidelines for Asking Questions with Authenticity

Here are tips to help facilitators translate the value of authenticity into action through effective questioning skills.

Build Group Ownership for Outcomes
Questions that work well are process enablers; they help to consolidate and strengthen the wisdom and power of the group.

2

As participants work together to ask and answer questions that enable them to solve a problem or develop a plan, they build ownership for a product or anticipated outcome. This influences the facilitator's role. On the one hand, if the facilitator plays too large a role in building the product, driving toward the outcome or influencing how it develops, group ownership suffers and participants may blame the facilitator if things don't work out the way they expect. On the other hand, they may give the facilitator too much credit should things work out well. Either way, group ownership of outcomes suffers.

Minimize Self-Deception About a Process

At the heart of authenticity is a refusal to engage in self-deception. Facilitators can avoid deceiving themselves about how well a process is going by asking themselves, the workshop participants, planning committee members, and other stakeholders how they are experiencing a session.

• Ask participants (sensitively) about unclear messages or possible self-deception. For example, "It sounds as if there might be a statement behind your question; do you want to raise another issue?" Questions of this sort should constitute a gentle challenge to support disclosure; they should not intimidate or irritate participants.

• Be candid about your impressions of a session, as a way to initiate a discussion about how things are going ("This feels like we're getting bogged down in details. How do you feel?").

• Use a simple feedback form or tool to support participants in disclosing what they think or feel about a process. Then share a summary of the feedback with them as a starting point for making necessary changes.

• If appropriate, use humor (perhaps a cartoon depicting a difficult situation) to raise sensitive issues for discussion. Keep in mind that effective humor is never at someone else's expense.

Be Clear About Intentions

When observing a group, I have sometimes seen the tone shift positively when members realize that the facilitator is well intentioned, objective, and focused on clear outcomes and that she wants to ensure a positive and productive experience. This shift happens if you are clear about your intentions and participants encounter your authenticity—if they see that you are being yourself in a difficult situation.

Once this shift happens, you can even make an error in judgment and the group will still support you because they can see your positive intentions; they respect your sincerity.

Being transparent about your relationship with a client can help create a positive tone. You might say, "I've met with . . . and we have been clear that there's no predetermined outcome for this session. My role is to ensure a healthy process. If I stray into content, please let me know right away." Transparency about intention supports authenticity.

> Humor can be a powerful conduit to meaning. It is a way to convey otherwise unsayable truths about human existence. Like art, it reveals meaning by juxtaposing the obvious with the novel. Also like art, it frees the imagination through its ability to tear down boundaries and stereotypes.
>
> —*Terry, 1993 (adapted)*

Acknowledge Problems

Being authentic means acknowledging (to yourself and others) when things aren't going well. Sometimes this can take courage because the response may include critical feedback or have an unexpected impact on your agenda. You might say, for example:

Did I confuse you? How about if I try to give those instructions more clearly?

Let's change the approach here so that we are more focused on our objectives. How could we make this more meaningful for everyone?

Looks like this activity isn't working very well. What's happening?

Seems as if we're a little off track here. Is it just me, or is anyone else having similar thoughts?

Be Honest About Your Competencies

Be honest with yourself and with clients about where your abilities lie. If you haven't facilitated a certain type of consultation before and are unsure about what questions to ask, be candid with your client; tell him that you want to do the work and would like to team up with someone who has the experience and skill in effective questioning to do a good job.

If instead you are comfortable in an area that requires complex questioning and facilitation skills and would like to stretch yourself by moving into a more advanced area, you may want to consult with colleagues to get the additional support you need to expand into that area on your own.

Be Present; Tune In

Doing a centering activity prior to every session helps me focus on the process and be fully present. Here is an activity (see Figure 2.5) that helps me get in tune with myself and my relationship with a specific group in a particular setting. It only takes a few minutes and yields significant benefits. This activity is adapted from a Tai Chi meditation, the First of the Precious Eight.

With practice, this centering activity becomes fluid, calm, and balanced. I usually repeat it three or four times. Depending on what is happening in a process, I may do the activity at a break as well as prior to starting a process.

Customize this moving meditation to suit your body and mind. I find it works best if I visit the room beforehand and picture myself in the specific situation where I will be working. Given the practical realities of where facilitation happens, I usually end up doing the meditation in a stairwell or washroom, whichever is handy.

Hear Your Client's Perspective

When you sign on to do a piece of work, listen carefully to your client's understanding of the challenge. Make the work more than just another contract that includes a purpose, objectives, and some type of payment, voluntary or otherwise. Get inside your client's perspective to understand her concerns and misgivings, her hopes and dreams. As you invest yourself and your organization 100 percent in a contract, you crawl inside the lived experience of the client to appreciate all the points in the process for which exceptional outcomes depend on the right questions.

Operationalizing the Value of Authenticity

How operative is the value of authenticity as you use questions in a process? Think about what you do when facilitating a specific situation involving questions. For

I.

Stand with your feet flat on the floor and about 6 inches apart, hands relaxed at your sides and eyes focused on a specific point in the near distance. Visualize a positive experience as you facilitate the group you are about to work with.

III.

Bring your hands down together a few inches away from your face, maintaining a prayer position, making a "shh" sound as you exhale gradually through your mouth.

II.

Inhale through your nose as you lift your arms over your head in prayer position, focusing your eyes on a point in the near distance.

IV.

Inhale again gradually through your nose as you fold your fingers together and raise your hands, reaching up as high as you can while lifting to balance on your toes. Maintain your focal point in the near distance, visualizing a positive and productive experience with this group. Maintain your balance, holding your inhale as long as is comfortable.

V.

Release your hands as you exhale audibly through your mouth, spreading your fingers and making a "shh" sound as you bring your hands to your side, slowly returning your heels to the floor.

Figure 2.5. Tuning-in Activity.

each behavior in Figures 2.1 and 2.6, to what extent is the value of authenticity posted or operative?

- Posted = knowing that the value is important, talking about it, saying you believe it is vital to effective facilitation

- Operative = acting on the value regularly, integrating it in your facilitation practice continuously

2. Authenticity	Posted				Operative
a. Build group ownership for outcomes	1	2	3	4	5
b. Minimize self-deception	1	2	3	4	5
c. Be clear about intentions	1	2	3	4	5
d. Acknowledge problems	1	2	3	4	5
e. Be honest	1	2	3	4	5
f. Be present; tune in	1	2	3	4	5
g. Hear your client's perspective	1	2	3	4	5

To operationalize this value further, I need to

Stop doing: _____

_____

Start doing: _____

_____

Continue doing: _____

_____

Figure 2.6. Operationalizing the Value of Authenticity.

MUTUAL RESPECT

Asked to develop rules or norms for working together, most groups identify mutual respect as essential to a healthy process. To describe what they mean by mutual respect, they may say something like "Everyone is important" or "Each of us has something to contribute or we wouldn't be here" or "Let's make sure that we really listen to each other and try to understand perspectives that are different from our

1. Integrity	2. Authenticity	3. Mutual Respect
a. Maintain objectivity	a. Build group owner-ship for outcomes	a. Enable equity
b. Clarify confidentiality	b. Minimize self-deception	b. Clarify group norms
c. Be sensitive to con-flicts of interest	c. Be clear about intentions	c. Respect exchange times
d. Avoid collusion	d. Acknowledge problems	d. Encourage direct interaction
e. Ask questions fairly	e. Be honest	e. Be patient; whose silence is it?
f. Determine authorship	f. Be present; tune in	f. Respect the energy in the group
g. Address imbalances in power and information	g. Hear your client's perspective	

Figure 2.7. Core Facilitation Values: Mutual Respect.

own." These are all good general descriptions of mutual respect. Figures 2.1 and 2.7 give six specific aspects of mutual respect in questioning.

Guidelines for Asking Questions with Mutual Respect

Here are six strategies outlining specific steps to help facilitators act on the value of mutual respect in asking questions.

Enable Equity

Equity is an important aspect of mutual respect. More than the perception of fairness, it involves acting daily in a fair and unbiased way.

There is a tendency to think of equality and equity as the same concept. The dictionary defines *equal* as "of the same quantity, size, number, value, degree, intensity," and "having the same rights, privileges, abilities, rank, etc." *Equity,* on the

2

other hand, is defined as "justice, impartiality; the giving or desiring to give each person their due; anything that is fair." Equality can be quantitatively measured, whereas equity requires a more qualitative assessment of what is fair and just (Strachan and Tomlinson, 1996).

Facilitators can support equity by ensuring that both advantaged and disadvantaged individuals and groups have a voice—that all are heard and respected ("Who do we need to make sure is included in our discussions but may find it difficult to participate due to resource issues?").

Questions that draw people out and give participants an opportunity to clarify what they mean are important in supporting equity in a session (see Chapter Three). A facilitator might ask, "We're missing input from the back table; where do you stand in this discussion?" or "So far we have one view on the floor. What other perspectives are in the room?"

An equitable process is based on inclusion; it respects the views of everyone involved, even though they may not be reflected in a final decision. Become aware of questioning patterns you may be developing with a group, such as asking more questions of people on one side of the room, or accepting that responses are appropriate before checking with other group members.

> Equality focuses on creating the same starting line for everyone. Equity has the goal of providing everyone with the full range of opportunities and benefits—the same finish line.
>
> —*Bruce Kidd, in Strachan and Tomlinson, 1996*

Ensure that you offer everyone in the group equal opportunity to respond to questions. Equity and inclusion are important facets of mutual respect. Questions to ask yourself: "Do I have any personal biases that influence how I ask questions, such as unconsciously respecting men's answers more than women's or vice versa, or discounting the wisdom of people whose language is accented differently from mine?" "How does the questioning in this session respect the rights of everyone involved?"

Clarify Group Norms

Norms that guide how people work together in a group are often implicit and unspoken. By identifying, clarifying, and articulating norms or ground rules for participation in a process, a facilitator can help participants think consciously about how they relate to one another in support of what they want to achieve, thus moving their values into action.

As group or team members build ownership for their roles and how they work together, they usually take more responsibility for reminding each other about the importance of sticking to group norms, particularly in discussing controversial issues. Guidelines and sample questions for setting group norms are found in Chapter Four.

Respect Exchange Times

Exchange time is the period between when one person finishes speaking and another person begins (see Chapter One). Some people have extremely short exchange times. If two people are talking on top of one another during a conversation, there is little or no exchange time. Other people, whose style is more reflective, may need a much longer exchange time between being asked a question and feeling prepared to respond. I have found (to my chagrin) that exchange time may also be culturally specific. I now make sure that I adjust the amount of facilitation time required depending on cultural norms for exchange time.

Waiting for three seconds or more can have a positive effect in a session, such as more people responding and more focused responses occurring. In addition, facilitators who monitor exchange time tend to use more varied and flexible questioning strategies as well as fewer (and more focused) follow-up questions, which can result in more strategic thinking on the part of participants (conclusions extrapolated from Rowe, 1987, and Stahl, 1994).

As a facilitator, it is important to respect a variety of exchange times and encourage participants to do the same. Respect for exchange time supports mutual respect by encouraging participants who favor reflection to participate more in the discussion.

Encourage Direct Interaction

Once ground rules for discussion are in place, constructive dialogue among group members (without the facilitator involved) can promote mutual respect, foster a balanced and impartial climate, and result in conclusions and decisions for which group members feel strong ownership. Encourage group members to ask and respond to questions—without going through you as the facilitator—so that they can learn directly from one another and build respect for each other's competence.

Some groups move easily into facilitating their own discussion. If this does not happen naturally, try some practical ways to support direct interaction:

- After a question is asked, avoid directive body language—such as specific eye contact—so that group members can respond freely rather than on the basis of your inclination.

- Be direct about how you would like discussion to happen ("Go ahead: I'm going to listen and observe").

- Don't repeat unheard answers to questions; instead, encourage the respondent to repeat the answer more clearly or loudly.

- Nod and look at the whole group when a participant asks a question rather than suggesting who could respond.

Be Patient; Whose Silence Is It?

Asking a question is like serving a tennis ball: you use the question (racquet) to put the discussion (ball) into play. Once you have asked the question, the silence in the room belongs to the respondents. Wait until they return the ball to you before you lob it back again. With a little experience, a facilitator can feel when a silence shifts back.

> As a blind man, lifting a curtain,
>
> knows it is morning,
>
> I know this change
>
> —Roethke, 1975

If you jump into a silence prematurely to rephrase a question or ask a specific person to respond, you reduce the amount of time that participants have to think about the question. In addition, they may perceive you to be uncomfortable with silence, or unduly nervous, which can reduce your effectiveness.

Respect the Energy in the Group

Individual and group energy is contextual and based on a complex set of factors, many of which a facilitator may not be aware of. To respect and understand this energy, one needs to be in a participant-observer stance and listening sensitively.

- Encourage participants to ask questions as they surface (except perhaps during a formal presentation).
- Responding to questions in the context of a group process can be exhausting work. Pay attention to when people need a break, and be prepared to be flexible; their needs may not line up with the timing on the agenda.
- Whenever possible, avoid telling people that an answer will be given at another time ("We'll cover that tomorrow" or "That's not discussed until this afternoon"). As soon as the individual or group energy generates a question, the subject is on the table. If time restraints are a consideration, you may want to facilitate a brief response and then ask if participants would like to pursue the conversation later in more depth.

Operationalizing the Value of Mutual Respect

How operative is the value of mutual respect as you use questions in a process? Think about what you do when facilitating a specific situation involving questions. For each of the six behaviors in Figures 2.1 and 2.8, to what extent is the value of mutual respect posted or operative?

- Posted = knowing that the value is important, talking about it, saying you believe it is vital to effective facilitation

- Operative = acting on the value regularly, integrating it into your facilitation practice continuously

LEANING ON VALUES

People facilitate best when they know and act on their core values and are skilled and well prepared. The core values of *I*ntegrity, *A*uthenticity, and *M*utual respect are easy to remember ("I AM") and can help support a facilitator feeling unsure about what may be happening with a group.

3. Mutual Respect	Posted				Operative
a. Enable equity	1	2	3	4	5
b. Clarify group norms	1	2	3	4	5
c. Respect exchange times	1	2	3	4	5
d. Encourage direct interaction	1	2	3	4	5
e. Be patient; whose silence is it?	1	2	3	4	5
f. Respect the energy in the group	1	2	3	4	5

To operationalize this value further, I need to

Stop doing: _____

_____

Start doing: _____

_____

Continue doing: _____

Figure 2.8. Operationalizing the Value of Mutual Respect.

One of my first contracts as a facilitator was with a national coaching certification program in high-performance sports. Before its inception, most coaches emulated other successful coaches. If a successful Olympic swimming coach taught athletes to do the front crawl with a flat, closed hand moving through an S-curve underwater, then there would be a large number of coaches emulating that practice, often without understanding why they were doing it (that is, the biomechanical principles involved). Because these coaches didn't understand stroke mechanics, they couldn't correct individual problems with any specificity; they were limited to doing what they had seen someone else do.

Although there is much to learn from watching others use questions, imitating others also means imitating their mistakes. There is no one best way to facilitate, no optimal personality to imitate, no magic answer for how to support healthy group process and achievement of objectives. If you ask questions with integrity, authenticity, and mutual respect, even the most challenging situations will yield results that reflect these values.

2

3 Follow-up Questions

Follow-up questions are prompts that a facilitator uses after an initial question or during a discussion. They can do much more than expand and clarify a response or point of view. They can take conversation to a deeper level, bring forward examples that stimulate empathy and understanding, clarify complex issues, and plumb the edges and extremes of an idea.

With follow-up questions, participants know that you are genuinely interested in their perspectives. You also enable group development through self-disclosure. Drawing people out through follow-up questions sends the message, "Take your time; we're interested in what you're saying and want to hear your ideas."

The follow-up questions in this chapter apply to all five chapters in Part Two of this book. More specific follow-up questions are also included in those chapters.

A facilitator using follow-up questions generally prompts participants in five main areas (Figure 3.1).

Prompt for . . .

1. Clarification
2. Perspectives
3. Rationale
4. Options
5. Implications

Figure 3.1. Five Prompts.

PROMPT FOR CLARIFICATION

Interesting, dynamic, and challenging discussion depends on clear ideas. Facilitators often need to probe further for clarification of what someone is saying, or to elicit additional information, as indicated in these examples:

Are you referring to . . . ?

Can you restate that in your own words?

Can you say that in another way?

Could you be more specific?

I'm not certain what you mean by that.

Keep going. . . .

Let's take this one a little further.

Tell me more.

What do you mean by the word . . . ?

What do you think is the main idea here?

What is your main point?

And then what happened?

And then?

Do you have a story in mind that illustrates your point?

It looks as if people are keen to hear more. Could you expand a little on exactly how that happened?

Please go on. Your example is helping to clarify things.

Tell me more about this. How did it begin?

PROMPT FOR PERSPECTIVES

In facilitating discussion, ask from time to time and in an encouraging way if anyone has another point of view. When probing for perspectives, focus on being inclusive, gathering a number of points of view—rather than trying to find out which perspective is accurate.

Ask for an example or an anecdote to clarify a response whenever someone gives you a general answer to a question. Examples and anecdotes make a session more vibrant and immediate; they are the spice in the conversation, the hook that enables others to identify with a particular situation or experience.

Does anyone see something different in the report?

Has anyone else experienced a similar situation?

Have we included any biases or stereotypes with respect to race, culture, class, ethnicity, gender, etc., that we need to address?

How can we find out if this is correct?

How does your perspective compare to . . . ?

Is there anyone we haven't heard from who may have a different perspective?

Let's hear another perspective so that we can capture more than one point of view.

Reactions?

To what extent has this fear (idea, suggestion) become a reality?

Were there any other choices in that situation?

What are some other options here?

What assumptions about . . . are you making with that response?

What comes to mind when you hear this?

What do you suspect is going on here?

What else fits here?

What might someone from . . . say about this point of view?

What went through your mind when this was happening?

What's your perspective (opinion, take) on all this?

Would it be fair to say that you have a lot of confidence in that approach? (*Variation:* Would it be fair to say that you are still questioning this approach?)

PROMPT FOR RATIONALE

In some processes, the reasons people support one position rather than another and the various types of background information and evidence are instrumental in decision making.

Are you aware of any work that has been done to support your position? If so, where can we find it?

How comprehensive is the background documentation on this item?

How was this argument developed?

How will we know that we have drawn the right conclusions?

If you just had a minute to make your case for this approach, what would be the top three items to mention?

Is there any evidence that supports a different perspective?

Is there someone we could contact who is doing leading-edge research in this area to make sure that we are considering all the evidence available?

Sounds like you did a lot of background work to get to your opinion. What influenced you the most?

What additional information do we need to help make a case for this approach?

What evidence would support this conclusion?

What is the best evidence on this topic? Where can we find it?

What made you think of that?

What new information would persuade you to change your mind?

What sort of bias do you think our approach has?

PROMPT FOR OPTIONS

Generate a full range of options to ensure that you are taking an inclusive approach and capitalizing on participants' experience.

Is there an option you would suggest if there were no limits on resources?

> Prompt: What would you suggest if you had no resources?

Is there anything about this option that you can't live with?

Think big and creative. What are all our options?

What alternatives do you have in mind?

What do you like most about this option?

What do you see as the most important challenge here?

What is another right answer to address this concern?

What other options did you explore?

What suggestions can you offer based on these comments?

Where else have you used this approach? How did it work?

Which approaches seems to support a win-win solution here?

Who else do you know in a similar situation? What did they do?

PROMPT FOR IMPLICATIONS

Understanding the implications of ideas helps to focus a discussion on session objectives.

Can we afford to live with these consequences?

Can you say more about that approach and what its impact might be?

Does this mean that . . . ?

Does this suggestion sit comfortably with you, or are you squirming in your seat?

How does this approach fit with our company values?

If we take this action, is what you are preparing a guaranteed result or just a possibility?

Is that a common use of the term . . . ?

Sounds like you see some long-term difficulties if we take this approach. Is this a fair comment?

What are the potential consequences for us in terms of . . . ?

> Prompt: What difficulties might these consequences cause?

What are the pros and cons of each approach?

What might happen if we took this option?

What other factors might influence what happens next?

Here is a humorous take on follow-up probes (Figure 3.2):

Passive	"Hmmm . . . I see. . . . " (deadpan expression)
Responsive	"Really? Thirty-three lovers? You seem to have led an interesting life. . . . " (smile, nod, raised eyebrow, eye contact)
Negatively responsive	"What a fickle woman you are!" (frown, scowl, avoidance of eye contact)
Developing	"Tell me more. Are you bragging or complaining? Why so many? What things do you most appreciate in a lover?"
Clarifying	"That's one and a half a year on the average; do you have affairs in sequence or concurrently? Do these men know about each other?"
Diverging	"And yet you claim to be in the forefront of the feminist movement. . . . Do you also know men merely as friends?"
Changing	"Okay, now tell me about your interest in Renoir paintings."
Involving	"Hey, baby, who y'got in mind for number thirty-four?"

Figure 3.2. Eight Follow-ups.
Source: Adapted from Ken Metzler, *Creative Interviewing: The Writer's Guide to Gathering Information by Asking Questions.* Published by Allyn & Bacon, Boston, MA. Copyright © by Pearson Education. By permission of the publisher.

WHAT TO ASK WHEN

4 Questions for Opening a Session

In opening a session, the main challenge for a facilitator is to create a positive climate that supports participants in achieving their objectives.

Climate is what it feels like to be in a particular setting. A positive climate in a facilitated session is one in which participants find:

- Permission to be themselves

- Pleasure and accomplishment in what they are doing

- Protection from negative dynamics

PROCESS FRAMEWORK

The opening part of a process supports participants in shifting their thoughts away from daily life and into the session, its purpose, and outcomes. The right questions create an opportunity for people to get to know one another, set some norms for working together, and clarify expectations (Figure 4.1).

The example that runs through this chapter uses this process framework to set questions that support positive climate setting for a scenario involving:

- A one-day workshop on team development

- A team that has been together for eighteen months

- Twelve people on the team

Figure 4.1. Process Framework for Opening a Session.

- Two significant issues to address

- Thirty to forty-five minutes allotted to opening questions

You have decided with the client that the purpose of the opening session is to give people permission to relax and be themselves in the session, share some personal information related to the agenda, and understand each other's hopes and concerns for both the session and the long-term challenge of working together well (Figure 4.2).

Although (as mentioned in the Preface) the questions in this chapter are designed for verbal interaction during a session, they can also be adapted to written formats.

Permission

Pleasure

1. **Getting to know one another**
   "We've been together for eighteen months now and have had a chance to get to know one another pretty well. If you think about our team as a give-get group, what is one thing that you enjoy giving or contributing to the team? What is one thing you would like to get more of or receive from the team?"

2. **Clarifying expectations**
   "Given our agenda, what needs to happen at this meeting for you to leave saying, 'That was a really satisfying and well spent day'?"

3. **Building commitment**
   "When it comes to our ground rules, what did we do particularly well at last month's team meeting? What could we focus on more today, given the nature of our agenda?"

Protection

Figure 4.2. Process Framework for Opening a Session: Sample Questions.

GUIDELINES FOR QUESTIONS TO OPEN A SESSION

Opening questions serve a session in many ways. The guidelines given here support facilitators in creating questions that work hard for them during an opening session.

• If you are facilitating an in-company meeting where everyone knows everyone else, use your insider knowledge to select questions that reinforce corporate values (for instance, reviewing company-meeting norms and adding one that focuses on challenges specific to the meeting).

• Opening sessions vary in terms of the amount of time available for introductions or climate setting. Sometimes (as with a three-hour meeting involving forty people) there is little or no time other than for stating one's name, location, and how one is involved with a particular project.

• Pace your opening questions so that the timing is right given the length of the overall session—say, ten to fifteen minutes for introductions for a three-hour session, forty-five minutes for introductions for an eight-hour session, or two hours for introductions in a three-day session.

• Relate your opening questions directly to session outcomes so that participants can experience the link between the questions and their productivity during the process. This builds ownership for expected outcomes. For example, "In light of our objectives, what would make you feel really good about this meeting?"

• Set questions that support each participant in making a positive initial impression ("What was your first positive experience earning money?").

• Play to participants' strengths by creating opening questions that enable all of them to feel included as legitimate members of the group ("Which part of this project interests you the most? Why?").

• Record responses to questions (perhaps writing them on a flipchart or using an e-display mechanism) so that you can revisit them at some later point in the process.

• Consider risk carefully. Some meetings and workshops need to begin with low-risk, nonthreatening questions that enable people to share personal information and build rapport in a comfortable setting. Other meetings and workshops may begin with high-risk questions that enable disclosure on issues and rapidly drive the agenda toward action. Consciously design an appropriate degree of risk in your opening questions.

• Select questions that let participants disclose their concerns, anxieties, and potential areas of disagreement in a nonthreatening, safe, and relatively low-anxiety setting ("What is one hope or one concern you have in relation to this meeting?").

• Use questions that enable participants to make the transition from their day-to-day reality into that of the session ("What did you have to do to clear your desk and make it here today?"). Such questioning can work particularly well for an in-house meeting.

• Have one question that assists participants in establishing a support network to sustain them after the session is over ("What is one thing you would like to learn from someone else at this session?").

• Generate a range of perceptions and perspectives so that all participants feel included: "There are a number of perspectives out there in relation to the potential success of this merger. Let's list as many as we can."

• Avoid an icebreaker in a warm climate. Icebreakers work when there is ice—a hard, cold surface that requires some melting or breaking to smooth your passage to wherever you are going. You don't need one if people in the group are comfortable with one another or can see where they are going and have the confidence to figure out how to get there. Participants may resent a getting-to-know-you game or other warm-up technique if they can't make an obvious link between the game and the objectives of the session. Instead of a game, consider asking a question with some risk in it that pushes people to think about the issues to be discussed.

• Inquire about experiences that relate directly to your objectives. Do not encourage a long description of academic credentials, previous job experience, or publishing credits. For example, "What is one learning experience you have had in the past few years that relates to this issue? Describe what you learned, in a single short sentence."

• Use the final question as a link into the next part of the agenda: "What is one thing you want to get out of this session that relates directly to what you are doing now at work?"

QUESTION BANK

Participants benefit from a supportive structure in forming a group (Tuckman, 1965). They need to know that the session is well organized, someone is responsible for getting things moving, there are an agenda and objectives, and they are valued for what they can contribute to the process.

Whether you are enabling participants to meet people for the first time or starting a team development workshop with people who know each other fairly well, effective questions can help participants find the motivation and ownership required to work with others and get the job done (Figure 4.3).

Figure 4.3. Getting to Know One Another.

Getting to Know One Another

Here are questions focusing on people learning about one another by sharing personal information and work experience. Adapt them depending on the extent to which people are acquainted with one another.

Focus: Sharing Personal Information

Complete this sentence: "My ultimate destiny is to. . . ."

Describe a fairly ordinary experience from your past that has come to be significant for you. What meaning did you take from this experience?

If you could change one thing about your education to prepare you better to work with our company, what would that be?

> Tip: By starting a question with "If you could . . . ," you open up possibilities for people.

If you could start a new political party, what would it be called, and why?

In a single sentence, describe one thing in your life for which you are thankful.

> **Tip: Limiting people to a single sentence encourages them to focus their thoughts.**

In adult education terms, an "a-ha" is a significant learning. What is one a-ha you have had about working in this organization? Please state it in a single sentence.

Most of us climb a number of metaphorical "mountains" in our lives. What is one mountain you climbed, and what did you learn from that experience?

Think about first impressions. What two words (to describe yourself) would you like people to think when they meet you for the first time? (*Variation:* What two words or phrases would people use to describe you?)

What do you do outside of work that helps you relax during stressful times at work?

What gift, experience, or unique contribution do you bring to this project?

What interests do you have outside of work that contribute to your effectiveness on the job?

What is a major change you have made at some point in your life that overall has had positive results?

> Prompt: What is a major change you have initiated that overall has had less-than-positive results?

What is a question that you are thinking about a lot at this point in your life?

What is one nonwork interest or activity of yours that most people here may not know about?

> **Tip: This works well with group members who know each other and those who don't. How you ask this question—verbally and nonverbally—determines how safe people feel in responding. Try using humor**

and give an example. We have had responses that range from "collecting spiders" to "reading romance novels."

What is one thing in your life that you are looking forward to over the next year or so?

What kinds of people make a positive first impression on you?

> **Tip: Try some questions as sentence completion, for example, "The people who make a positive impression on me are. . . ."**

What motivated you to work as a teenager?

> Prompt: What motivates you to work now?

What would you like to know about one another?

> **Tip: Brainstorm some suggestions with the entire group—three to five minutes—and then make up a list of two or three questions for each person to consider.**

When you meet new people, what is the first thing you want to know about them?

Where are you from? Tell us one interesting fact about your home town.

> **Tip: Put a plasticized map on the wall and give participants colored dots to place on their geographical location. Colors can represent different reasons for participation: one color for a national perspective and another for a regional perspective.**

More questions on sharing personal information:

_____

_____

_____

_____

_____

Focus: Exploring Work Experience

(The word *work* is used here in its most general sense—that is, paid, volunteer, in the home, however the participant views it.)

Describe the earliest positive experience with earning money that you can recall.

> **Tip: This question can be useful in opening a planning session for sales-people.**

How did you make your first dollar? (*Variations:* Customize this question to suit your objectives; for example, "What are the first words that come to mind to describe your initial experience as a trainer in conflict management?" or "What was your first memorable experience as a manager?")

How do you make a difference in your workplace?

How does your organization show that it cares about its employees?

How have you been involved with this project up to now?

If you could change one thing about your work situation, what would that be?

If you could have any job you wanted in any type of company anywhere in the world, what would that be?

In your experience, what part of being a supportive team member requires courage? (*Variation:* Substitute other words for *courage.*)

Most people want to work in an environment where they feel happy about what they do. When do you feel happy at work?

Think about this group as a whole. What words would you use to describe us?

> **Tip: Using this question after some basic introductions creates a shared perception of the group that can come in handy later on as you work together to achieve objectives. Be sure to check out individual percep-tons with the group.**

What are you doing now in relation to the projected outcomes for this process?

Which aspects of your work in policy development are most satisfying?

Prompt: Which are most frustrating? (*Variation:* Substitute other areas of work for policy development.)

What do you do to escape the pressures you experience at work?

What do you enjoy contributing to this team?

Prompt: What do you enjoy getting from this team?

What do you find most rewarding about your involvement in this area?

Prompt: What do you find most challenging about your work in this area?

What is it about your organization and the work you do that you appreciate the most?

Prompt: What is it about your organization and the work you do that causes you the most irritation?

What is one memory you have of your work experience that you enjoy revisiting?

Prompt: What is one memory you have of your work experience that you don't enjoy at all?

What is one stereotype that you have heard about people in our industry?

Prompt: In what sense do you agree or disagree with this stereotype?

What is unique about the kind of work you do?

What is your most important value about working in a team situation?

What other work-related group processes (such as planning, training, team development) have you been involved with that are similar to this one?

What three things do you do most in a typical day on your job? Be specific so that we know exactly what it is that you do.

What was your primary motivation in coming to work for this organization?

> Prompts: To what extent has this motivation been fulfilled? What motivates you to continue working for this organization?

What words or phrases come to mind to describe your supervision style?

When it comes to managing, who was your most important teacher?

> Prompt: What is one important thing you learned from that person? (*Variation:* This question works well with a variety of substitutions for the word *managing,* such as "selling," "communication," or "planning.")

When you think about what it feels like for you to work in this organization, what song or movie comes to mind?

> Prompt: What made you think of that?

More questions on work experience:

_____

_____

_____

_____

_____

_____

_____

_____

4

Clarifying Expectations

It takes time to clarify process objectives and outcomes. No matter how clear the purpose of a session may seem to you as facilitator, participants often interpret the purpose in a variety of ways on the basis of their experience. The questions given here help to clarify participant expectations by discussing hopes and concerns and confirming objectives and outcomes (Figure 4.4).

Focus: Understanding Hopes and Concerns

Given the purpose of this workshop, what needs to happen to make it a successful event for you?

If you were facilitating this workshop, what is one thing you would make sure happened?

I signed up for this program because. . . .

Is there anything special you would like to learn about or do on this project that contributes to your career goals?

Think about this initiative as a mentoring opportunity. What would you like to learn?

> Prompt: Whom would you like to partner with?

Think about this project as a potential investment. What aspects of the project would encourage you to invest in it?

This committee has been in place now for three years. From your perspective, what has the committee accomplished?

> Prompt: In what areas has the committee been less successful?

What advice do you have for the workshop facilitator?

What are the potential opportunities, benefits, and costs for each of us as a result of working together collaboratively?

What do you think needs to happen to make this process productive? (*Variation:* Substitute other words for *productive,* such as "fair," "enjoyable")

4

Figure 4.4. Clarifying Expectations.

What do you want to be thinking as you head out the door at the end of the day?

What excites you about this realignment process?

> Prompt: What causes you concern about this realignment process?

What has our . . . said lately that you think is important to our discussions?
  (*Variation:* Substitute various positions in the organization depending on the focus of the process.)

What is one assumption you are making about this project that you're not sure other stakeholders share?

What is one hope you have for this session?

> Prompt: What is one concern you have?

> **Tip: Be clear about what you mean by a hope and a concern. Questions that ask for opposites tend to get similar responses—for example, "This is my hope and my concern is the opposite of that." (Variation: Substitute "dream" and "nightmare" in the question.)**

What is one question you would like answered by the end of the day today?

> **Tip: Record and post participants' questions so that you can check them off as they are answered during the session.**

What is one obvious area of agreement among everyone here that could give us a good jump start on building further agreement?

What is the best thing that could happen for our organization as a result of this workshop? Begin your response with "We. . . ."

What motivated you to take this job?

What motivates you to be involved in this project?

What needs to happen during today's session to keep you engaged on this initiative over the long run?

Which parts of this process interest you the most? Which parts are relatively uninteresting to you?

Would you like any special training or coaching to participate fully in this project?

More questions on hopes and concerns:

_____

_____

_____

_____

_____

4

Focus: Meeting Objectives and Outcomes

As a new department is formed *by merging your two work units,* what aspects of how work was done *in your unit* would you like to make sure is kept in the new department? What aspects would you like to change? (*Variation:* Adapt this question to various situations by substituting other phrases for the words in italics.)

Dr. . . . will be joining us tomorrow morning to make a presentation on. . . . Given the purpose of this meeting and her expertise in this area, is there anything you would you like me to pass on to her about what you want to hear during her talk?

From your perspective, what is the most important outcome this project will achieve?

Given your position in the organization, what changes would you like to see that could benefit the organization as a whole?

In a single, brief sentence, in your own words, and from your perspective, answer the question, "Why are we here?"

In what ways are we already on our way to achieving our outcomes on this initiative?

Please review the objectives posted on the wall. Do they seem realistic given the amount of time we have? Any changes, additions, deletions?

> **Tip: Confirming objectives builds ownership for the process and outcomes of a session.**
>
> Prompt: The fourth objective refers to "shared interests and problems of researchers in your field." From your experience, what interests and problems would you like to see addressed at this workshop?

Think about the end of this process. What legacy would you like to see in place for your organization?

This committee has been in place now for three years. What would you like to see the committee accomplish over the next three years?

What are you expecting from others during this session?

> Prompts: What do you think they are expecting of you? What are you expecting of yourself?

What exactly do we mean when we say our organizations are "collaborating" on this initiative?

> Prompt: What are the expectations for how we will be involved, who will make decisions, and where leadership will reside as we work together on this initiative?

What is a burning (key, important) question that we must address to be successful?

What needs to happen to make this workshop successful, from your perspective? (*Variation:* "What would success look like or feel like to you?" or "How will we know that we have been successful?")

Where might you like to provide leadership on projects like this one?

More questions on objectives and outcomes:

_____

_____

_____

_____

_____

_____

Building Commitment

The commitment of participants to the outcome of a process builds with mutual support for shared norms or ground rules, the opportunities they have to air or discuss their points of view with one another, and the sense they have of contributing to outcomes. (See Figure 4.5.)

Figure 4.5. Building Commitment.

Questions in this section focus on group norms and building ownership for outcomes.

Focus: Developing Group Norms

On the basis of your experience, what are the three most important characteristics of effective meetings?

> Prompt: How can we ensure that our meeting has these characteristics?

Given who is engaged in this process, what is your best guess about one or two values that we all share?

> Prompt: How might we test whether these conclusions about values are accurate?

Given your experience with this group, what is one thing that everyone could do at this meeting to ensure its success?

How can we ensure that stakeholder roles and responsibilities are clear, understood, and specific to our initiative?

> **Tip: Thinking about specific aspects of their past focuses participants on hindsight learnings and the need to apply them in the present.**

How can we ensure that the agendas for our meetings are developed with all of our interests in mind?

How can we revisit how we are working together?

How will we make decisions?

If a dispute arises, how will we address it in support of our objectives?

Language is an important part of how we will communicate while we are working together. How will we develop a common language for key terms and acronyms?

On the basis of your experience, what are the three most important characteristics of effective meetings? How can we ensure that our meeting has these characteristics?

Think about what we want to accomplish through this session. Then think about yourself and others participating in this session. What are three or four basic rules of the road or guidelines for working together that would support us in being successful as we work together?

> **Tip: You may want to give a couple of examples, such as coming back from a break on time, and putting electronic devices on Silent or Off during a session.**

We have a full agenda and some specific outcomes to achieve. I see a key part of my facilitator role as working with all of you to create a positive and productive climate, keeping us focused and on time. This might involve. . . . Are you comfortable with this?

Prompt: Are there other aspects of how we work together that you think we should pay special attention to?

We have a range of participants in this session. Some are actively advocating a point of view and others are inquiring about perspectives on this issue. What are some guidelines that will help us balance advocacy and inquiry throughout this workshop?" (Ross and Roberts, 1994, pp. 253–259)

What are all the ways in which people can sabotage sessions like this one? Think about your school years, between the ages of about thirteen and seventeen, and make a list of all the things you used to do (or saw others do) that would sabotage the possibility of a successful learning (meeting) experience.

Tip: Turn this sabotage list into a set of norms by discussing their opposites.

What are our ground rules or guidelines for raising concerns?

What are some boundaries that we can set to keep us focused on our specific objectives and prevent us from trying to be all things to all people?

What are the top two things you think children should be taught about conflict management?

Tip: Avoid asking a question such as, "How did you learn about conflict while you were growing up?" as this may surface painful memories of abuse or parental conflict for some participants.

What is a ground rule that you have had at other meetings that you would like to have for this one?

Prompts: What is a ground rule that you have had at other meetings that you would not like to have for this one?

What is a watchword for this meeting that will help make it successful?

What is one really helpful thing that you learned about working with others that has stayed with you? How could that learning be useful for how we work together during this meeting?

What is one rule you learned in grade school that you wish everyone would follow during sessions like these?

What is one thing that we can do to support each other in achieving our objectives?

What is one thing you do not want to see happen in this session?

What will this group look like at the end of its task, if people are really working well together?

More questions on group norms:

_____

_____

_____

_____

_____

_____

Focus: Building Ownership

Describe a proud moment in relation to your work on this issue.

How do you evaluate how successful a meeting is?

How would you describe this group to a friend?

How would you describe your role in this group to a friend?

If you could change one thing about how this board functions, what would it be? (*Variations:* Replace *how this board functions* with "how we work together," "how we do our work," "how feedback is given," "how we are paid," and so on.)

To what extent are you engaged in supporting this workshop? (*Variation:* "To what extent are you engaged in supporting the potential workshop outcomes?")

What are you certain about with respect to being a member of this group?

> Prompt: What are you uncertain about with respect to being a member of this group?

4

What do you think is unique about this group? (*Variation:* Substitute another word for *unique*.)

What do you think needs to happen at this meeting to ensure its success?

What is one thing you have learned about this area since we met last?

What motivates you to do a good job for this organization?

> Prompt: What would motivate you to make a 150 percent commitment to this workshop process?

What needs to happen during this process to ensure that you are fully committed to the outcomes?

What two values do you have that you think most people in this group share?

> Prompt: What two values of yours do you think some people in this group may not share?
>
> **Tip: Be sure to check out these inferences about values with group members.**

What would make you feel really good about this process?

When you think about this group as a whole, what are our biggest opportunities?

> Prompt: What are our biggest challenges?

You have been asked to design a welcome mat for people coming into this workshop room. What message would you put on your welcome mat?

More questions on building ownership:

_____

_____

_____

_____

_____

COMMON CHALLENGES

These real-life examples explore opportunities for conscious use of questions when opening a session.

When Time Is Short

Challenge: I recently facilitated a five-hour workshop with fifty participants for a national charitable foundation. The purpose of the session was to review regional statements of mission and values (for twelve regions) and bring them together into a common national statement for the federation. As part of our preparation, we developed a background document that compared current jurisdictional statements.

There were about fifteen people in this session who were new to the organization and had not met one another, so we wanted to do meaningful introductions but in a short period of time. It didn't work out quite the way I imagined; we spent too much time up front on introductions, even though it did help the group to gel somewhat. What would you ask in a situation like this, and how would you ask it?

Response: If introductions are essential and time is short, it is important to share that information with the group and ask them to keep their comments very brief. Post the questions you want them to answer at the front of the room. Brief two people about the challenge ahead of time, and ask them if they will role-model what you want at the front end.

Facilitator script: "It's important for us to get an overview of who is in the room. Given the time we have to accomplish our objectives, let's spend twenty seconds per person doing some very brief introductions through two questions. Although our time is short, the final question is important, so please take a minute now to think about what you want to say." [Pause and present the two questions—see options below—keeping them in front of participants, on a flipchart or projector.] "I've asked a couple of people to model this approach, and then we're off. Altogether we have twenty minutes maximum for this activity."

First question: Name, affiliation, location.

Second question: Here are some questions that have worked well in similar situations. Using these suggestions as a starting point, make up a question to fit your workshop objectives.

One hope or one concern you have in relation to this workshop; you can't give both.

What is one item in the front of your mind as we start this retreat?

What is one thing that makes meetings like these successful?

What motivated you to accept the invitation to participate in today's discussions?

Given your perspective, what is the most important item on today's agenda?

Once you have been around the room on these two questions and have recorded people's answers, it is good to process them overall in the room by asking a question such as, "Now that we have been around the room, what stands out for you about today's workshop, according to what you have heard?" Be prepared to customize your agenda on the basis of this activity.

Opening a Workshop on a Specific Topic

Challenge: I often facilitate sessions that focus on a specific topic such as leadership, mentoring, or benchmarking. This means that during the opening part of the session I have to think about how to introduce the topic and also begin to drive toward objectives and outcomes at the same time. What do you suggest?

Response: Here are questions that are helpful in sessions that focus on a given topic. The examples are listed under specific topics but can be adapted for use with other areas.

Leadership

Think about your experience to date as a senior leader in your organization.
What is a key learning you have had about organizational leadership in your working life? State your learning as a commandment.

> Tip: When leaders respond to a question like this one, there is enough risk involved to support group development and enhance ownership for the outcomes of the session.

What is a challenge that your organization [or another organization you know] is currently facing in relation to leadership?

> Tip: The option in brackets encourages disclosure without breach of confidence.

What is at stake in our country in relation to corporate leadership at the national level?

When should our [insert sector] leaders say no instead of saying yes or pretending that they don't see the challenge?

Mentoring

If you were starting your career again, in what topic area would you request mentoring?

You have been asked to act as a mentor to a new employee who is a young, recent graduate of an MBA program. What are the top two pieces of advice you would give this young person to support his success in your company?

Ethics

From your perspective, what are the ethical dilemmas involved in this issue?

> Tip: Explaining words such as *ethical* ensures that the responses will tie into your objectives.

When questions about ethics arise in your sector, what area seems to surface most often?

Performance Management

If you could change one thing about how this company rewards employees—other than increasing financial rewards—what would it be?

Team Development

What is your most important contribution to this team to date? What do you get from this team?

Program Review

What is one good thing about this program so far? What is one not-so-good thing about this program so far?

Workplace Feedback

What is one thing about ethics (or service, marketing, and so on) in this organization that you are proud of? What is one thing about ethics (service, marketing, and so forth) in this organization that needs to be improved?

Perspectives and Challenges

When you look at this situation from the perspective of a . . . what are the main challenges?

Problem Definition

Describe the two biggest problems in this project as catchy newspaper headlines.

4

Priority Setting

What are your top two criteria for funding projects in this area?

Consensus Building

Where do you think the greatest area of agreement is with respect to resolving this issue?

> Prompt: Where do you see the greatest area of disagreement?

Financial Success

What does it take to be successful financially in this company?

What was your first paid job?

> Prompt: What would you like your last paid job to be?

Values Clarification

Are you materialistic?

> Prompts: If so, how? If not, how?

If you saw someone stealing something from a store, would you intervene?

> Prompt: Why or why not?

In what ways are you a conformist?

> Prompt: In what ways are you a nonconformist?

Personal Development

If you could accomplish one significant thing over the next year, what would that be?

If you won the lottery, what would you do with the money?

What is a risk you feel comfortable taking that others whom you know might feel awkward in taking?

What is one bad habit that you have broken during your lifetime?

What qualities do you want in a friend?

Opening a Series of Workshops

Challenge: When we facilitate several workshops or meetings that happen over a period of time, in a limited series or involving scheduled reunions of a group, the opening questions are often based on hindsight about what has happened in previous sessions. Can you suggest some questions that work well in this situation?

Response: One approach is to focus on what was learned previously as a way to encourage participants to think about what they want to learn at the new session. For example: "What did you get out of your last meeting with group members?" or "What do you want to get out of this meeting?"

Another approach is to focus on the personal responsibility of individuals in taking ownership for a productive and enjoyable experience as a group member:

At our last meeting, we set a number of norms for working together to ensure that the session would be productive and enjoyable. Given your experience at our last meeting, which of these norms do you think is most important in ensuring a positive experience for you this time around?

What did we do well at our last meeting in terms of group norms?

> Prompt: What do we need to focus on this time around?

At a recent graduate school alumni reunion for organizational change practitioners, participants from twenty-five years of classes were asked to sit in groups according to their graduating class, develop a group response to three questions, and record their responses creatively in flipchart space on the wall. Each class had its own section of a twenty-five-year timeline spread out along two walls. There were two flipchart pages for each class.

The questions were:

What was going on in the business world when your class was in session? (key events or incidents)

Describe briefly a defining moment or a highlight for your class.

Provide a word, phrase, symbol, picture, or drawing that reflects the essence of your class.

This opening activity took about three hours for all the classes to complete, including process time in plenary. It yielded thumbnail insights into each class over a twenty-five-year period, helped classes build ownership for their unique experience as they presented their overview to other classes, and enabled them to see snapshots of the school's entire history in an afternoon.

The activity seemed to have just the right amount of risk to support rapid group development during this first reunion for alumni. Most of the professionals at this graduate school are comfortable with a fairly high level of risk in terms of group process and would have been disappointed by an opening activity that didn't challenge them in some significant way.

4

Several classes were explicit about the intense frustration they experienced during a period of upheaval and disorganization in the university's administration. Other classes celebrated what was for most of their students a life-changing learning experience. One class talked about the lack of bonding in a year when expectations about intellectual intimacy were not realized. A recent graduating class used this activity to explore why their experience was not of the quality they had expected.

As a participant-observer at this event, it seemed to me that these questions elicited powerful, insightful responses that enabled plenary group development and brought closure to the past while opening up avenues for future learning. The questions also fed directly into the objectives for the reunion, which were focused on learning from the past and building for the future. As each class presented its perspective on the past, it was enlightening to watch other classes run the gamut of responses: joy, frustration, concern, surprise, confusion, disappointment, and mutual support.

Loosening Up a Tight Group

Challenge: I am going to facilitate a weekend strategic planning retreat for a very successful, conservative, primarily male law firm that prides itself on its establishment image. What questions can you suggest for opening the first evening of this workshop for thirty partners?

Response: Planning retreats for professional firms may include the usual strategic planning objectives as well as a combination of team development issues for the firm, partner conflict management problems, and questions related to the future direction of the firm. The sooner the facilitator can set and implement norms for how issues will be identified and addressed, the better the planning process proceeds. You can gather considerable information about the firm prior to the retreat and then use that information as a basis for questions during the opening session.

Here are some sample opening questions that have worked well for a variety of professional firms in areas such as law, medicine, accounting, education, and dentistry. These questions all depend on workshop participants having received, prior to the workshop, a confidential and anonymous report on interviews or questionnaires completed by the firm partners. Be sure to ask questions that include just the right amount of risk and disclosure for encouraging participants to begin building ownership for the overall process.

Questions Related to the Report

How did you feel when you finished your first reading of this report?

The objectives for this session were developed prior to this report. After reading this report, do the objectives for this session still seem reasonable, or do we need to fine-tune them?

This report provides a snapshot your firm that is based on interview questions that the planning committee developed with us. For how long has this been a snapshot of your firm?

What common threads do you see weaving through this report?

What do you like most about the image of your firm? What do you like least?

What do you think someone from another firm would conclude about your firm after reading this report?

What is there in this report that makes you feel optimistic about your future?

> Prompt: What is there in this report that makes you question the future of the firm?

What stood out for you on your first reading of this report?

> Prompts: Are these conclusions accurate? Would you suggest that a new hire read this report?

Additional Questions

From your perspective, what is a key element in your vision of this firm three years down the road?

Think of a planning retreat that you participated in that was a success from your perspective. What made it successful? Think of one you participated in that was not successful from your perspective. What made it unsuccessful?

> Tip: Turn the responses to this question into a list of norms for working together.

What is one norm for working together as partners that you think needs to be in place to ensure that this workshop is successful?

What is one piece of information related to the future of the firm that you think everyone should keep in mind during this planning session?

What needs to happen at this retreat to make it successful from your perspective?

4

5 Questions for Enabling Action

Many facilitated discussions are directed toward clear and specific outcomes requiring action on the part of participants. Whether the purpose of a group is to do strategic planning, team development, account planning, project implementation, policy development, or revision of a production schedule, action is usually required of the individuals involved, as well as for various subgroups and for the larger organization or community.

PROCESS FRAMEWORK

By using the "What?—So what?—Now what?" process framework of Figure 5.1 to guide questioning and stimulate discussion, facilitators can play a key role in keeping people on track and enabling action.

As Figure 5.1 suggests, this process framework has three main question categories. Usually the facilitator describes the discussion topic or task (content) clearly in terms of objectives: "Our purpose here is to review and finalize the mission. Let's take a look at the summary of focus group results and see what it tells us about our mission statement."

A *notice* question from the What? category (in the Question Bank pages of this chapter) leads participants to make some observations about this content ("What stands out for you in this report about our mission statement?").

Figure 5.1. Process Framework for Enabling Action.

A *meaning* question from the So what? category asks participants to consider or reflect on how their observations fit with their current situation and values ("What do these observations tell us about how this mission statement fits with our organizational values?").

An *application* question from the Now what? category asks participants to think about possible action steps or behavior change ("How do you want to change the mission statement?" "Which key words or phrases should be changed?").

The What?—So what?—Now what? process framework is handy and easy to remember. As Figure 5.2 illustrates, you can use these three questions to frame a specific task or discussion and enable it to move toward action.

Process frameworks are flexible; the arrows in these figures are not rigidly defined. Some questions are general notice questions ("What stood out for you in this report?") and would be very close to the "Notice" end of the *Observations* arrow in Figure 5.2. A question such as "What potential problems jumped out at you on first reading?" is closer to the "Meaning" end of the *Observations* arrow.

This framework appeals to a variety of learning styles (Kolb and Fry, 1975; Johnson and Johnson, 1996; Marks and Davis, 1975; Jones and Pfeiffer, 1980;

Figure 5.2. Expanded Process Framework.

Argyris, 1970, 1985; Gaw, 1979, 1980, pp. 3–8; Wheeler and Marshall, 1986). Several writers have explored experiential learning in terms of behavioral change; some of the questions in this section come from these articles, but most are from our experience in the field. For another perspective on experiential learning related to research paradigms, see Reinharz (1981). For yet another perspective, see Stanfield (2000a). People who like to observe will find their strengths in the notice (What?) questions, those who are adept at reflection and abstract conceptualizing will enjoy the meaning (So what?) questions, and those who are skilled at taking action will find their niche in talking about applications (Now what?).

Knowledge is produced in response to questions. And new knowledge results from the asking of questions. . . . Once you have learned how to ask questions—relevant and appropriate and substantial questions—you have learned how to learn and no one can keep you from learning whatever you want or need to know.

—Postman and Weingartner, 1969

GUIDELINES FOR QUESTIONS TO ENABLE ACTION

The What?—So what?—Now what? process framework has a clear focus on action, outcomes, and accomplishment. The guidelines presented here support facilitators in selecting or developing questions that enable action, a focus on outcomes, and a sense of accomplishment among participants.

• Start with where the group is. In some discussions, participants begin with "So what?" questions and then go back to "What?" before moving into "Now what?" The questions are interdependent; throughout the framework, use the order that makes sense for your particular situation.

• If a discussion gets bogged down or there is too much silence, it is often because the discussion is stuck in an inappropriate part of the framework. For example, you may have asked a "Now what?" question about applying information from a video or a presentation at a time when the participants were just starting to notice things ("What?") about it. Or you may be facilitating the values clarification part of a strategic planning meeting with a group that includes a lot of people who are impatient about getting to the action steps. Pace the process framework to suit the group.

• Be sensitive to group dynamics in facilitating questions in this framework. On the one hand, complex situations may require more discussion during the What? part of the framework so that participants can take the time to understand a topic completely. If the What? part is clearly understood, the other two parts often proceed more efficiently. On the other hand, in a difficult situation involving conflicting perspectives on key issues, you may notice that group members resist decision making by spending an inordinate amount of time in the What? and So What? phases. Either way, it is the framework you lean on to make decisions about when to move participants forward in what way and toward what end. It usually sounds something like this: "We've spent about thirty minutes exploring the report, your reactions to it, and how the recommendations fit with our objectives. I'm suggesting that we spend the rest of our time thinking about how to apply our conclusions to next steps—the Now what? part of our agenda. Are you comfortable with moving on now?"

• Learning styles have an impact on your success in using this framework. If you have a lot of participants whose learning style leans toward taking action, they

5

may want to skip the So what? questions or spend less time on them than people whose learning style leans more toward reflection and generalization. Use your experience and input from the group to pace and order your questions, ensuring that you spend an adequate amount of time in each area on the framework, but not so much that you bore or distract people who have strengths in other learning styles.

• In working through the framework, normalize the variety of perspectives in a group as well as the potential for conflict. For example, "There are usually more than one or two perspectives on this issue. What other points of view can we raise here?" or "Conflicting perspectives are what make discussions like this one interesting. Who has another view?"

> The effective facilitator is situationally responsive. He or she guides any particular group of participants to find learning that is meaningful and testable for them, regardless of whether it fits with the author's or facilitator's conceptual scheme. In other words, the process is trusted to unfold and evolve. The ideal facilitator does not lead the participants to conclusions but rather stimulates insights and then follows what emerges from the participants.
>
> —*Gaw, 1979*

• The "So what?" part of the framework asks people for their opinions about how things fit together. Questions on this part of the framework that begin with *how* are usually less intimidating than those that begin with *why* (see the section in Chapter One on skills for conscious questioning). A *how* or *what* question asks for a description, whereas a *why* question tends to ask for a reason or explanation. Many participants don't like to explain their actions or give reasons in a group. If required to do so, they can become defensive and stay silent—or make up what they perceive to be an expected response. For example, a gymnastics coach asked an athlete, "Why did you slow down at the big turn?" The athlete looked down and said nothing. When I asked her later about her lack of response, she said, "No matter what I said, I knew it would be wrong." When I asked the athlete (in a nonthreatening tone), "What were you thinking about as you came up to the big turn?" she responded, "My line of approach seemed off and I wasn't sure I could complete that landing safely."

> *Avoid asking* why *when feelings run high.*

• Setting a clear purpose and objectives for a process is essential in formulating What?—So what?—Now what? questions. The more clarity you have about these basics, the more your process framework can support you in making up questions on the spot during group discussion.

QUESTION BANK

Whether you are developing questions well ahead of your session or making them up on the spot, the process framework for enabling action ensures that you are prepared and have a conceptual framework for moving forward.

"What?": The *Notice* Questions (Observations)

What? questions raise awareness; they ask participants what they think and feel about something.

Here are sample What? questions for use in the process framework of Figure 5.3. They could pertain to someone thinking about an experience, or they could follow a presentation, video, report, discussion, or structured activity.

As we begin this first strategic planning session, what is in the front of your mind with respect to our organization?

Any surprises here?

> Traditional aboriginal teachings seem to suggest that people will always have different perceptions of what has taken place between them. The issue, then, is not so much the search for "truth" but the search for—and the honouring of—the different perspectives we all maintain. Truth, within this understanding, has to do with the truth about each person's reaction to and sense of involvement with the events in question, for that is what is truly real to them.
>
> —*Stanfield, 2000a*

Figure 5.3. "What?" Questions.

Has anyone else has had a similar experience?

How did that feel?

> Prompt: Who had a similar reaction when listening to this speaker? Who had a different reaction?

How involved were you in this presentation?

> Prompt: Were you riveted, or thinking about things in the office, or doing a grocery list?

In "buzz groups" of three, share your impressions of this presentation.

So, what's your gut reaction to this approach?

> **Tip: This question could be used after a controversial or stimulating speaker. You could replace *gut reaction* with other phrases such as "initial response" or "intuitive response."**

> In order to grow in awareness, the individual may have to stop the action, pause and center directly on himself. What am I feeling at this moment? What is happening within me right now? What is my mood? Do I feel tensions in my body? If I listen carefully, can I actively be in touch with the source of my discontent? What do I want? What do I prefer? How many different levels of awareness can I reach when I am alone? Can I describe each feeling? What thoughts and feelings stand out? Concentrated attention and focusing are initial steps through which awareness develops.
>
> —*Moustakas, 1974*

What are the first words or phrases that come to mind after seeing that film?

What caught your eye in this report?

What did you bump up against in this report?

What did you hear that you don't already know?

> Prompt: What did you hear that you need to hear again?

5

What did you notice?

What did you observe when you did that?

What general feeling does this video leave you with?

What happened there?

What is another way to say this?

What is happening here?

What jumped out at you when you saw this for the first time?

What kinds of feelings did you have while watching this video?

What parts of this presentation did you relate to most?

What potential problems or challenges jump out at you in this report? (*Variation:* Substitute other words for *report*, such as "approach" or "plan.")

What stood out for you?

What struck you about that?

More What? questions:

_____

_____

_____

_____

_____

_____

"So What?": The *Meaning* Questions (Reflections)

These So what? questions (Figure 5.4) are grouped into three focus areas: relevance and fit, organizations, and individuals.

Focus: Relevance and Fit

After hearing (experiencing, discussing) this, has your opinion changed about our approach?

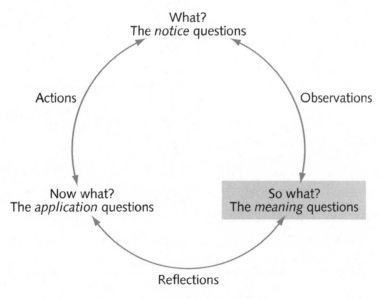

Figure 5.4. "So What?" Questions.

Can you recognize your situation here?

Describe this report from the perspective of. . . .

Do you see any patterns here that relate to our situation?

> Prompt: What are some examples of similarities or differences?

Does this approach (film, report) remind you of anything in your past experience?

Does this make sense to you?

> Prompt: In what way?

Does this video make any assumptions about race (or gender, age, class, religion) that have an impact on its conclusions?

Given what you have heard, which groups external to us are relevant to our work? (*Variation:* Replace *groups* with "factors" or "individuals.")

Given your perspective, what are the main points of view in this presentation?

How are contradictions and dilemmas addressed in this report?

How are people with special needs affected by this approach?

How do you account for that happening in this situation?

How does this compare with what you expected?

How does this line of thinking relate to our objectives?

How does this relate to what we were talking about in the last session?

How does today's session relate to our last meeting?

How does what we are discussing here fit with our mission? (*Variation:* Replace *mission* with the department's purpose, or the unit's key objectives.)

Is this what you thought might happen?

On a scale of 1 to 5, where 1 is low and 5 is high, what relevance does each of these items have for your workplace?

Think about this report in terms of implications for our organization. What three main headings would you make to describe implications?

What central themes about . . . can we pull from this?

What concerns does this raise for you?

What did you learn or relearn from this discussion?

What do you notice about the characteristics of your group in relation to the recommendations in the report?

What does all this mean to you?

What has been done about these problems so far?

What is your dream for this area in ten years' time?

What key points can we pull from this presentation?

What options were available in this situation that were not discussed?

> Prompt: Why do you think these options were not put on the table?

What other projects are you aware of that have objectives and issues similar to this one?

> Prompt: What can you learn from those projects?

What parts of this report or presentation are relevant to your organization?

What questions can you come up with for this speaker that would help us understand this area better?

What was significant for you in this approach?

> Prompt: Why was it significant?

Where's the meat in all this?

Why does this feel so important to you?

Would you engage this speaker for your group?

> Prompt: Why or why not? (*Variation:* Substitute "use this video," "hold this discussion," "circulate this report" for *engage this speaker.*)

5

Would you recommend this video to other groups?

> Prompt: Why or why not?

More So what? questions focused on relevance and fit:

_____

_____

_____

_____

_____

Focus: The Organization

Assume that you are doing a report for your internal newsletter. What headline would you write to catch people's attention about the importance of this report for our organization?

Does this approach fit with how your organization does things?

Does this video support your own experience? Please explain.

How does this relate to your situation at work?

How does this report fit with what you already know about this issue in your organization?

How is this result significant for your organization?

How realistic is this plan, given available resources?

If you could offer some feedback to one of the consultants in this film to improve her interpersonal skills, what would you say and why? (*Variation:* Replace *improve her interpersonal skills* with other options.)

If you were building a scrapbook on this subject for your organization's archives, what memorable incidents or defining moments would you include?

What additional questions does this presentation raise for you as a senior manager in your organization?

5

What are some differences between the reality presented in this video (report, presentation) and the reality in your organization?

> Prompt: What are some similarities?

What are the consequences of doing nothing in your organization in relation to the conclusions of this meeting?

What aspects of this problem are nonnegotiable in your area of the organization?

What core organizational values would support what we have been discussing here today?

What did you find most useful about this presentation?

What do you predict would happen in your department if you tried the approach suggested in this report?

What does all this suggest to you about best practices in this area?

What does this presentation or document suggest to you about the current situation in your group or organization?

What does your organization want to get out of all this? What do you as an individual want from this?

What generalizations can you make about your organization in relation to the information in this presentation?

What guiding principles or rules of thumb do you see operating here?

> Prompt: Are they appropriate for your organization?

What issues in your organization are similar to those discussed by the speaker?

> Prompt: What issues are different?

What parts of this morning's discussion have a potentially positive impact for your organization?

What potential consequences does this approach have for your organization?

5

What values about the workplace are demonstrated in this video that you would like to either take on or avoid?

When and how do you deal with issues on this topic in your organization?

Which result of this report has the most meaning for your organization?

> Prompt: What makes this result meaningful?

Here are the three key points this morning's speaker will be making. During this presentation, please rate your organization on each of these key elements.

> **Tip: Put this question on a worksheet for note taking during a presentation.**

More So what? questions focused on organizations:

_____

_____

_____

_____

_____

_____

Focus: The Individual

Does this approach remind you of anything in your experience?

How do these suggestions fit with your own projects in this area?

How does all this fit together for you?

If this were your presentation, how might you have done it differently?

What (if any) significance does this learning experience have in your life?

> Prompt: If it is significant, how so?

What are the implications of this discussion for your immediate work environment?

What are these ideas associated with in your mind?

What do you see as the complicating factors in this approach for someone in your position?

What does this information suggest to you about yourself and those you work with?

What kinds of things mentioned in this article have you already tried?

What sort of real-world, day-to-day problems or issues in your life come to mind when you reflect on this presentation?

What values about leadership stood out for you in the film?

> Prompt: Who saw something different here?

What were your hopes and expectations when you first joined this group?

> Prompt: To what extent have they been realized?

Which of these guiding principles for organizations are also applicable to families?

> Prompt: How are they applicable? Examples?

5

Critical insight often occurs unexpectedly. The moments when people break through habitual ways of interpreting some idea, action, or social structure cannot be predicted in advance. It is not uncommon to be thinking about some aspect of one's life and experience a sudden flash of insight concerning an apparently unrelated area.

—*Brookfield, 1987*

More So what? questions focused on individuals:

_____

_____

_____

_____

_____

_____

"Now What?": The *Application* Questions (Actions)

Application questions (Figure 5.5) lead to personal and organizational change by building ownership and through planning and implementation. The Now what? questions given here are grouped into four main areas: personal change, organizational change, building ownership, and operational planning and implementation.

Focus: Personal Change

As a result of today's meeting, what is one thing you could start doing? stop doing? continue doing?

> **Tip: Use these three questions as the basis for a workshop journal.**

In your journal, name three changes you could make in your family life that would reduce the amount of distress in your life today.

Let's look back at what you wanted when you completed the needs assessment for this session. Did you get what you wanted from this process? What are your next steps?

On the basis of your experience and the conclusions in this report, what tips would you give to someone new in this area?

Please note your top two areas for desired change on the page provided. Then put it in the envelope, seal it, and address it to yourself. I will mail it to you in three months as a reminder of your commitment.

Think big. What are all your possible choices here?

What did you learn here that you would like to transfer into your situation back home?

> Prompt: What support do you need to make that transference happen?

> **Tip: "Back home" could be taken to mean in the workplace or in the person's family situation. Be explicit.**

Figure 5.5. "Now What?" Questions.

What is one attitude you saw that you would like to have as a leader?

> Prompt: How could you start to make that happen?

What is one thing you learned here that applies to your life outside your workplace?

> Prompt: What are the implications of this learning for personal change?

What is one thing you will do differently as a result of participating in this session?

> Prompt: What will you do first to get started?

What is one thing you would like to do more of in your work situation?

> Prompt: What is one thing you would like to do less of in your work situation?

What possibilities do you see now that weren't obvious before?

What were your hopes and expectations when you first joined this group?

> Prompt: To what extent have they been realized?

What learnings are you taking forward out of this experience?

More Now what? questions focused on personal change:

_____

_____

_____

_____

_____

_____

Focus: Organizational Change

Can you recall any situations similar to this that your organization has faced in the past?

> Prompt: If so, how could we adapt, build on, or learn from whatever was done last time?

How could you apply what you have learned in this experience to your organization?

How relevant were these discussions to your day-to-day work situation?

How threatening will this change be to our employees?

> Prompts: Why might this change be threatening? How can we help prepare employees for this change?

What conditions will you need to create in your organization so that you can successfully implement the changes you want to make?

What is one simple step you could take when you go back to your office that would have a positive impact in this area for your organization?

> Prompts: When will you take this step? How will others in this group know that you have done it? What will be the benefits of doing it?

What is one thing you heard about here that you don't want to see in your organization?

> Prompt: How can you prevent it from happening?

What was your original organizational objective for participating in this process?

> Prompt: Have you met it?

What will you have to do to make this work in your environment?

More Now what? questions focused on organizational change:

_____

_____

_____

_____

_____

_____

_____

_____

5

Focus: Building Ownership

Are there any existing or potential interpersonal tensions in our organization that could get in the way of our achieving our goals?

> Prompt: How can we address them now to prevent problems later on?

117

At what point in this process should we consult with others who are less directly involved but who could have an impact on how we implement this?

How are you going to build ownership for making some changes in your department in relation to what you have learned here?

How can we build "mind share" for our account plan with other areas in our organization?

How can we transfer ownership for the plan from this small group to the entire organization?

Is there anyone who was not at this meeting but should be involved in the future?

What approaches can we take that will motivate people to collaborate with us on the next steps?

What initiatives are you currently involved in that could be affected by or contribute to the success of these changes?

> Prompt: How might you follow through on this information?

What is your most optimistic view of how this could turn out?

> Prompt: What is your most pessimistic view?

When you begin to implement these changes in your organization, where do you expect the trouble spots to be?

> Prompt: What can you do to ensure you are prepared to address potential problems?

Who is already on board with this approach?

> Prompts: Who is partly on board? Who is not on board at all? How do we ensure we have the people we need on board? What action can we take to get them on board?

Who is providing leadership in your organization with respect to initiatives affiliated with this one?

> Prompt: How could we get them involved in supporting our work in this area?

Who may be excluded as a result of this new approach? What can we do (if anything) to accommodate these people?

Whom should we acknowledge or thank for their contributions and involvement to date?

More Now what? questions focused on building ownership:

_____

_____

_____

_____

_____

Focus: Operational Planning

From what you have learned here, what could you do personally to ensure that the changes you are making will go as smoothly as possible?

Do you need approval from anyone to proceed with implementing your plan?

> Prompt: If so, how can you get that approval?

How reasonable are our timelines for implementation? (*Variation:* "How can we determine the best way to pace the implementation of this plan?")

If you could get any one key person you wanted to participate in helping with the implementation of this project, whom would you pick?

> Prompts: Why would you suggest that person? If that person isn't appropriate (for any reason), is there someone else or a combination of other people who could provide the same insights, energy, and experience?

5

In a year's time, how will we know whether we have been successful?

Now that we have made this decision, what are the implications for our team (organization) over the next three months?

Prompt: Six months? year? two years?

Think about the structure of our organization. How will it support what we want to do?

Prompt: How might it hamper what we want to do?

What are some dos and don'ts to follow in your organization while applying what you have learned here?

What are the primary outcomes that we want?

Prompt: What are our secondary outcomes?

What do we need to pay attention to as we move forward?

What driving or supportive forces will enable you to implement this plan?

Prompt: What restraining or inhibiting forces could be a barrier to implementation?

What have we learned about implementing plans in previous situations in our organization?

Prompt: How can we use this information to help pave the way for this plan?

What information do we need to be able to demonstrate that we have achieved our goals?

Prompt: To whom should we communicate this information?

What would a human resource capacity audit tell us about how to take the next steps?

> Prompt: Who can contribute positional power to support implementation with respect to this challenge? (*Variations:* Substitute other capacities for *positional power*, such as "personal experience" or "access to financial resources.")

What is one thing that each of us can do to support implementation of this approach?

What is our Achilles heel on this project?

What is the best sequence for the main categories in this plan?

What kind of human and financial resources do we need to support this work?

What lessons have you learned elsewhere that will be useful now that we are about to take action on this project?

What political dynamics are you likely to encounter when implementing the plan?

> Prompt: How could we anticipate and address these dynamics?

What potential is there in this plan to increase tension among key stakeholders?

> Prompts: What potential is there in this plan to decrease tension among key stakeholders? How do we want to accommodate the potential for tension as we implement this plan?

What skills and experience do we have in this group that will support implementation of this plan?

> Prompt: What additional skills and experience will we need if we are to be successful?

5

What specialized skills or knowledge do you require to be successful in implementing this plan?

Where does accountability lie with each of us? (*Variation:* Substitute other words for *accountability*, such as responsibility.)

Who are our top three customer groups?

> Prompt: What could we do to serve each of them better?

Who in our organization has the authority to act on this plan?

Who will be responsible for communication in relation to the changes being made? (*Variation:* Substitute other responsibilities for *communication* such as "monitoring and evaluation" or "updating.")

Whose influence do we need if we are to get this done?

More Now what? questions focused on operational planning:

_____

_____

_____

_____

_____

_____

COMMON CHALLENGES

The real-life examples presented here explore opportunities for conscious use of questions in enabling action.

Supporting Action After a Meeting of a Network or Coalition

Challenge: What questions can I use to bring an action-oriented ending to our provincewide green environment network meetings?

Response: Sometimes it's helpful to teach the What?—So what?—Now what? framework as a way to raise awareness about how an agenda is organized to enable action during a network meeting. This usually takes about ten minutes. In general, participants appreciate learning the framework and can see uses for it in many situations, both personal and professional.

Once participants understand the framework, you can use questions such as these to close your network meeting and support next steps.

What?

What stood out for you during this meeting in terms of our current emphasis on . . . ?

So What?

How does this observation fit with our current goals for this area?

Now What?

What are the implications for us as . . . regarding what we have learned here today?

What is one thing we can all do as network members over the next month to support our network's current emphasis on . . . ?

5

Enabling a Structured Approach to Reflection and Action

Challenge: The groups I work with are not good at dialogue. After reviewing a report they argue, debate, and posture, but they don't really explore new learning or action. Can you suggest some questions that would help with this problem?

Response: Create explicit and focused questions that guide discussion through the What?—So what?—Now what? framework. Create opportunities for as much air time as possible, building agreement in stages from pairs or trios to the larger group.

> We are not good at balancing advocacy and inquiry. Most of us are educated to be good advocates. While there is nothing wrong with persuasion, positional advocacy often takes the form of confrontation, in which ideas clash rather than inform.
>
> —Stanfield, 2000a

What?

In trios: What main conclusions did you see woven throughout this report? Share individual impressions and come to agreement on the top two conclusions.

So What?

Does your experience as a senior manager support these conclusions? Note a couple of examples to illustrate your point of view.

On a scale of 1 to 5, where 1 is not in agreement at all and 5 is completely in agreement, indicate the degree to which your organization is in line with these conclusions. Please give a rationale for your choice.

Now What?

What is one change you could make in your organization to build on the conclusions in this report and that would have a significant, positive effect on employees?

Discussing and Making Decisions That Affect Organizational Policies

Challenge: We are discussing the impact of new tobacco legislation at an upcoming senior managers' meeting in our national, heart health NGO (nongovernmental organization). This legislation will arrive on our desks the day before we need to discuss it. What are some questions we could use to explore the legislation and guide our discussion and decision making?

Response: Contact participants the day before the meeting to request that they read the legislation prior to discussing it the next day. Do what you can to ensure that everyone has had the time to read the legislation, reflect on it, and make notes about potential implications (for example, postpone other meetings and activities). You may want to devote an additional five or ten minutes at the beginning of the meeting for people to review their notes and jot down their responses to the first question before initiating discussion.

Use the What?—So what?—Now what? process framework in this chapter to guide development of questions.

What?

Given your experience with this issue, what are the first words that come to mind to describe this document?

What jumped out at you on your first reading?

So What?

What stands out for you about this potential legislation when you think about our new capital project?

How will this bill have an impact on society at large? Do any potentially positive social benefits (such as increased employment) outweigh any concerns we may have?

Which of these impacts (if any) will be beneficial for us? How?

> Prompt: Which of these impacts will cause us problems? How?

Now What?

What are our options for action in relation to this legislation?

Which of these options will we take?

What is the first step to ensure a positive outcome for our NGO?

Applying Research (Knowledge Translation)

Challenge: I work at a national think tank that produces research papers for review by senior leaders in organizations at international conferences. In the past, we simply did the research, produced the paper, and then convened workshops and conferences for discussion purposes. Our customers want more now. They are emphasizing the importance of knowledge translation (closing the gap between what we know and what we do) in their work situations. What are some questions we could ask to stimulate discussion and help our customers apply the conclusions in these research papers to their organizations?

Response: It sounds as if you (the think tank) are moving from presenting information to encouraging your customers (senior leaders in organizations) to explore relevant content and apply it to their work situations. Depending on the size of the group involved, the questions given here, all based on the What?—So

125

what?—Now what? framework, may be directed to people in various ways (large group, small group, consideration as part of a task, preparation for a presentation, and so on).

What?

Describe your first reaction after reading this report.

> Prompts: Did anyone else have this reaction? What is this reaction based on?

If you could add a section to this paper, what would it be called?

What is onße question that surfaced for you after reading this paper?

So What?

Does this report take into consideration the social and political context in which your organization is functioning today?

If you acted on the key conclusions in this paper over the next six months, what risks would surface in relation to your bottom line?

If you could have a private lunch with the author of this paper and ask her anything you wanted, what are two questions you would ask?

How do the conclusions of this report reflect your experience?

> Prompt: How do they not reflect your experience?

Is your experience similar to that of the authors, or different from theirs? Please explain.

Think about leaders you respect in your area of work. How would they view this report?

> Prompts: What parts of this report would you like to discuss with them? Why?

What does your experience and intuition say about the relevance of this research to your organization?

What sort of real, back-home issues in your life are related to what is discussed in this paper?

When you think about organizations like yours, would these recommendations do more good than harm?

> Prompt: How do you know?

When you think about the kinds of issues your organization is facing now, do these conclusions seem relevant?

Would publication of this report make a difference in your area of work?

> Prompt: Why would publication matter or not?

Now What?

On the basis of this research, what is one small thing you could do to bring significant benefit to your organization?

What impact do you think the conclusions in this research report could have on your field over the short run?

> Prompt: What might the impact be over the long run?

What is one insight you gained from reading this paper and discussing it with your peers?

> Prompt: How might this insight serve as a catalyst for change in your organization?

What truths about your organization are reflected in the conclusions and recommendations in this report?

> Prompt: How could you act on these conclusions and recommendations to improve how your organization functions?

5

Workplace Stress: Personal Change

Challenge: I am leading a stress management workshop for union stewards in my company. This is a very, well, stressful topic in our macho environment. Participants have just completed a questionnaire on their personal stress level. How can I support them to feel comfortable about disclosing their scores and working on strategies for enhancing how they manage stress in this environment?

Response: First, normalize the range of scores on the instrument and the fact that everyone experiences and deals with stress differently. Second, emphasize that there is no way to avoid stress; it is a normal, predictable part of every person's life. Third, disclose your own scores on the instrument for a time in your life that was very stressful.

Another potentially powerful approach is to plot individual scores anonymously on a wall chart when people are not in the room. This visual approach can be an effective stimulant for discussion.

With either approach, you can then work through the What?—So what?—Now what? framework with questions such as these.

What?

What is one thing that stands out for you when you look at your results?

What strikes you about this score?

So What?

What does this score say about the amount of distress you are experiencing in your life now?

> Prompts: Is it manageable? unmanageable?

What is one thing that you see other people doing in relation to time off and stress management that you would like to do in your life?

> Prompts: What is preventing you from doing so in your life? What supports do you have in your life in relation to this goal?

What is your score?

> Prompt: Does this score make sense to you given your current personal and work situation?

Now What?

Given your situation at home, what is one thing you could do now or over the next twenty-four hours that would make a positive difference in relation to anxiety and tension in your life?

What is the first thing you will do personally to get started on this change?

Whom can you count on to support you in making this change?

> Prompts: What does this person need to do to be supportive of your decision? How will you talk to this person about the changes you want to make?

5

6 Questions for Thinking Critically

Effective questioning is an essential component of critical thinking—an examination of how and why things are done the way they are. Critical thinking leads to deeper understanding and is based on open-mindedness, active inquiry, and increased awareness and sensitivity.

Critical thinking is an essential skill in a situation involving complex problem solving. It doesn't necessarily move toward action per se, but it does move toward a clearer understanding of a situation—an essential prerequisite for determining effective action. Facilitators encourage critical thinking in a variety of situations, where:

- Participants are challenging why things are done the way they are

Critical thinking involves getting beneath the surface.

- Participants could be more sensitive to the situation of others or more alert to their own feelings and those of others, especially in a situation involving an imbalance of power

- There is a need to hear a variety of views on an issue, develop optional strategies, or explore more than one way of doing things

- You want to raise awareness among participants that how things are done is closely related to a specific context and period in time

> Come on now, we're going to go build a mirror factory first and put out nothing but mirrors for the next year and take a long look in them.
>
> —Bradbury, 1950

Critical thinking stimulates group members to learn together. It encourages participants to explore their experiences, ideas, assumptions, and beliefs about a topic as a way to discover their own truth in relation to that topic.

The first step in moving toward critical thinking is to ask thoughtful questions: "Reflective skepticism is not outright cynicism, nor is it contemptuous dismissal of all things new. It is, rather, the belief that claims for the universal validity and applicability of an idea or practice must be subject to a careful testing against each individual's experiences. It is being wary of uncritically accepting an innovation, change, or new perspective simply because it is new. It is not to be equated with resistance to change" (Brookfield, 1987, p. 22).

As an illustration, the Art Gallery of Ontario (Canada) uses critically reflective questions to encourage patrons to consider works of art in a variety of dimensions. Here are two questions that appeared in an exhibit (in March 2001) on naked bodies.

"Who decides what beauty is? Are naked bodies always erotic? Who says what it is to be feminine or masculine?" (near paintings and sculptures by masters such as Jules Pacquin, Kees van Dongen, Auguste Rodin, Alberto Giacometti)

"Do women have to be naked to get into the Metropolitan Museum of Art? Less than 5% of the artists in the Modern Art sections are women, but 85% of the nudes are female." (on the 1989 poster "Guerrilla Girls" of a reclining female nude with a gorilla head)

6

> Commitment to the truth does not mean seeking the "Truth," the absolute final word or ultimate cause. Rather, it means a relentless willingness to root out the ways we limit or deceive ourselves from seeing what is, and to continually challenge our theories of why things are the way they are. It means continually broadening our awareness, just as the great athlete with extraordinary peripheral vision keeps trying to "see more of the playing field."
>
> —Senge, 1990

PROCESS FRAMEWORK

The process framework for critical thinking in Figure 6.1 includes questions in four main areas. For each area, three perspectives are provided: the individual, the team or organization, and the broader context. Although these four areas can be thought of sequentially in terms of how a session might flow, in practice they can emerge in various ways at different times.

With regard to these questions and activities, there are no right answers (though there might be many wrong answers). The questions are not meant to be tests. Their value should be in the self-searching they inspire and the discussions they provoke.

—*Scholtes, 1998*

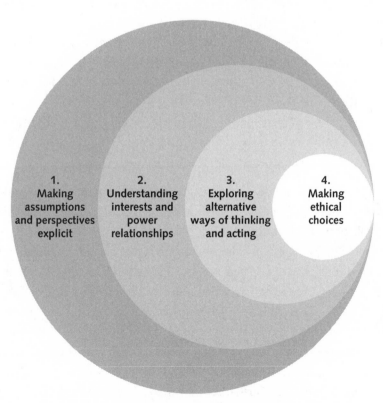

6

Figure 6.1. Process Framework for Thinking Critically.

The value of a process framework is that it imparts a basic structure while enabling a facilitator to adapt to evolving dynamics. The process framework in the previous chapter focused on enabling action; the focus in this chapter is on reflection that may not result in any specific decisions for action. The purpose of a session may simply be to reflect on a situation and understand stakeholders' perspectives.

Although (as mentioned in the Preface) the questions in this chapter are designed for verbal interaction during a session, they can also be adapted for written feedback forms.

GUIDELINES FOR QUESTIONS TO ENABLE CRITICAL THINKING

The guidelines given here support group facilitators in using the process framework to develop a supportive climate for critical thinking.

Taking time to reflect on a situation in detail and engage in thoughtful dialogue is not something that everyone is comfortable with. Some people (such as those who work in emergency situations) may think that questions of this sort are a waste of time—that they explore the obvious—and one should get on with taking action. Other participants (such as those who live in a spiritual community or are philosophically oriented) may find time spent in reflection to be essential in creating a strong basis for moving forward.

• Develop a comfortable climate for participants in which candor and critical reflection are important norms for working together. A supportive atmosphere gives people permission to think critically (see Chapter Four).

• As you develop questions for critical reflection, pay close attention to nuance in relation to your objectives. There is a fine line between insightful, directed questions that support discussion focused on outcomes and meandering or vague questions that don't seem to go anywhere. When it comes to critical thinking, participants must feel that the pace and focus of discussion is appropriate to expected outcomes.

• Support participants who ask difficult or awkward reflective questions. "These are important questions—they may make us feel uncomfortable, but that's probably a sign that we should be thinking about this"; "Let's explore this tension a little further—this usually leads to constructive discussion").

• Model critical reflection by being open to new perspectives, challenging assumptions, and welcoming diversity and other ways of thinking.

• Initiate critical thinking using both positive and negative events and situations. If you use only the negative, participants may conclude that critical thinking is a negatively based function. Instead, consider, for example, "Yesterday's meeting was efficient, fun, and very productive. What were we doing that made us so successful?"

• Explore the assumptions underlying various perspectives of group members ("When you state your position that way, what assumptions are you making?").

• Enable participants to disclose and discuss differences between how things are supposed to work and how they actually do ("This video presents an ideal situation for implementing organizational change. How does it look in comparison to the day-to-day reality of life in your organization?").

• Give participants an opportunity to reflect on what they are discussing through time for talking with others, reading articles, and so on.

• Move from specific to general. Participants usually grow more comfortable with critical thinking if you begin questions or discussions with a specific situation and then work toward broader implications. As an example, hold up a recent newspaper article about a protest that is linked in some way or another to the group and ask, "What would you protest publicly, in relation to the issue we are discussing?"

• Critical thinking involves going beneath the surface. Ask questions that clarify or expose whose interests are being served in a particular situation. Explore who stands to benefit or lose as a result of changes you may be considering.

• Most rewarding critical reflection involves risk. As facilitators, we are bound by an ethical imperative to point out to group members, learners, and clients the potential risk involved in various change efforts that might result from intensive critical scrutiny of a situation. Check your workshop design with your client or supervisor to ensure that she is comfortable with the risk involved in exploring questions that have a critical thinking element.

• Critical thinking takes time, particularly for those who are new to it. People need to test how ideas feel, exploring their assumptions and values in relation to approaches and positions. Slow the pace and ensure that you have adequate time in

6

> Once you foment, make time to ferment.
>
> —Mike Tomlinson

your agenda to support effective critical thinking so that people don't feel rushed. It takes time for participants to explore each other's interests and ideas and mature as a group into critical thinking on an issue.

• Know when to stop thinking and move toward action. Critical thinking can go on and on and take you to some very interesting places that lead nowhere. As a result, it can be a strategy, conscious or unconscious, to avoid making a decision or taking action.

QUESTION BANK

Whether you develop questions well ahead of your session or make them up on the spot, the process framework for critical thinking ensures that you are prepared and have a conceptual framework for moving forward.

Making Assumptions and Perspectives Explicit

Critical thinking enables participants to be aware of what other group members are thinking, what their assumptions are with respect to a topic being discussed, and how their perspectives and those of others fit or don't fit. The questions in Figure 6.2 help to make assumptions and perspectives more explicit in group settings.

Focus: The Individual

How do others perceive my expectations?

> Prompt: How do I know this?

What are the implications of your personal style in your role as a member of this task force (organization, corporation, group)?

What comes to mind when you hear the phrase *corporate loyalty*? (*Variation:* Substitute other phrases to surface individual perspectives in other areas.)

What do I know for sure about my perspective on this issue?

> Prompt: What do I know for sure about others' perspectives on this issue?

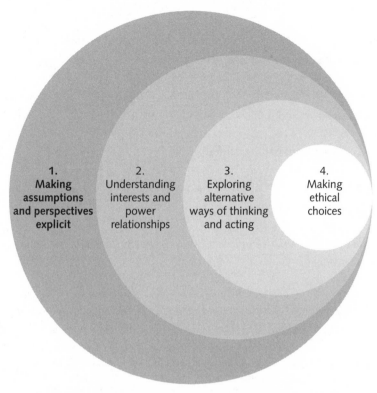

Figure 6.2. Making Assumptions and Perspectives Explicit.

What helped to shape your opinions about . . . ?

What is an unspoken assumption that you have about the outcome of this meeting?

What is my client's perspective on this issue?

> Prompts: If you can describe your client's perspective, ask: "How do I know this?" or "How can I confirm this?" If you can't state your client's perspective, ask: "Why don't I know this?"

I have often found that differences of opinion result from different sets of assumptions. To deal with these differences, one needs to examine the reality of the assumptions behind them.

—*Felipe Alfonso, Asian Institute of Management*

What is your bottom line on . . . ?

What kinds of activities in your day-to-day work make you feel good (or not good) about your current position?

> Prompts: Why do you feel good (or not good) about these activities? What could you do to feel consistently better about the work you do?

What kind of behavior makes you feel good about a supervisor?

> Prompt: What kind of behavior makes you feel uneasy or uncomfortable about a supervisor?

> **Tip: Develop the list of responses into a checklist on healthy behavior for supervisors.**

More questions about assumptions and perspectives focused on the individual:

_____

_____

_____

_____

_____

_____

Focus: The Team or Organization

From your perspective, what are the main characteristics of our organization's culture, our day-to-day practices, or how we do things?

> Prompts: Which of these practices are you most comfortable with? Which are you uncomfortable with? What factors in our environment have helped to shape these practices?

How do we handle the good times? the bad times? (*Variation:* Substitute words such as "dull" and "exciting" for *good* and *bad.*)

How often do you speak out on topics or issues related to your organization's mission and values?

> Prompts: Do you speak out with your own immediate team? with others in your professional community? in your larger community? What happens as a result of your comments?

Imagine that you have been asked as an external consultant to evaluate the performance of members of our board of directors over the past two years. What aspects of board performance would you consider?

> Prompt: Why?

Individual experiences in an organization often reflect broader organizational issues that must be addressed. What experiences have you had as a manager in this organization that point to broader organizational issues needing to be addressed?

The philosopher Nietzsche said, "There are no facts, only interpretations." What generally accepted facts about our organization do you think could also be seen as interpretation? Please explain.

The slogan "Think globally, act locally" [or some other slogan] is widely used today. Does it have any relevance for your organization?

> Prompts: Why or why not? What are some examples to support your position?

What are all the possible positions a person on your team could take on this issue?

What assumptions about how we work together need to be changed?

> Prompts: Would any of these assumptions take courage to address? How might this need for courage affect what we do?

6

What assumptions about our organization are at the heart of this approach (issue, decision)?

> Prompt: Do you agree with these assumptions?

What criteria should we use to determine who is involved in a task force on this issue?

What do you think the person responsible for . . . needs to hear from . . . to make sound decisions about the future directions of the organization? Summarize your input in a single sentence.

What is going on now in your organization that causes you to feel optimistic about the future?

> Prompt: What is going on now in your organization that causes you to feel pessimistic about the future?

> There's nothing more debauched than thinking.
> This sort of wantonness runs wild like a wind-borne weed on a plot laid out for daisies.
>
> Nothing's sacred for those who think.
> Calling things brazenly by name,
> risqué analyses, salacious syntheses,
> frenzied, rakish chases after the bare facts,
> the filthy fingering of touchy subjects,
> discussion in heat—it's music to their ears.
> —*Szymborska, 1995*

What is one aspect of your work environment that is stressful for you and your team?

Prompts: If you were in charge, what would you do to reduce the distress? How do you think this situation came about?

What two key events (critical incidents) stand out in your mind as defining (or being typical of) how your organization functions? Please explain.

What's your best hunch about what this organization will look like in three years' time if it continues with the current path and strategies?

When you think about the future of this company (group, organization), would you describe yourself as leaning more toward optimism or pessimism?

Prompt: Why?

More questions about assumptions and perspectives focused on the team or organization:

_____

_____

_____

_____

_____

_____

Focus: The Broader Context

Choose a newspaper, magazine, journal article, audiotape, or radio interview with a clear point of view and ask participants to consider these questions:

- Are these views supportive of or contrary to your own point of view?

- Do the opinions in the article reflect one or more points of view?

- Do you know of any important information that is not presented in the article?

- Does the information presented support the main points of the article?

- Does the language or terminology indicate any particular bias?

6

- How are statistics used in the article? Are the statistics valid or skewed?

- How legitimate is the information source?

- How is information used in the article? Does it support a particular point of view?

- What are your overall impressions?

- Who bears the costs of the views expressed?

- Who benefits from the views expressed? (Tomlinson and Strachan, 1991, p. 12)

Consider this quotation: "Asking awkward questions about the rightness of, and justification for, political decisions, actions, and structures is the focus of critical thinking about the political world" (Brookfield, 1987, p. 165). What questions need to be asked about racism in our country?" (*Variation:* Substitute other words and phrases for *racism*: "health care," "infrastructure support," "youth offenders," "access for people with disabilities," "misuse," "social support funds.")

How do the issues in our organization reflect current trends and concerns in society in general?

> Prompt: Does our response to this question support or hinder how we do our work? In what ways?

Give participants an article that includes statistics on an issue you are discussing, and then select questions such as these to stimulate a discussion about perspectives:

- Does this perspective we are discussing provide a model *of* the world (as you see things now) or *for* the world (as you would like things to be)?

- How might these statistics be interpreted by senior management in your organization? (*Variations:* Substitute for *by senior management in your organization* "by a minister in a fundamentalist church," "by a politician in the middle of a reelection campaign," "by the head of your local advocacy group on this issue," or "by a reporter for a tabloid newspaper.")

6

- What are all the ways our stakeholders (senior management, clients, allies) might interpret these statistics?

- What do these statistics mean to you? (Tomlinson and Strachan, 1991, p. 18)

What factors in our current environment are supportive of how we work together now?

> Prompt: What factors in our current environment are challenging how we work together?

What are the first words or phrases that come to mind when you hear the word *poverty*?

> Prompt: How do these initial words and phrases reflect your perception of this issue in our country? (*Variation:* Substitute other words and phrases for *poverty:* "crime," "older people," "wealth," "incompetence," "best practices.")

What are the popular perceptions about this issue in our country?

> Prompts: Do you agree with these perceptions? Why or why not? Whom do you know who shares these perceptions?

What are the underlying dynamics or forces at work here?

> Prompt: Is there anything we should be concerned about, given our situation?

6

What metaphors do you hear or see in the media in relation to this issue?

> **Tip: Give an example of a metaphor not related to the topic being discussed, such as couch potatoes, heartless industrialists, bleeding-heart liberals.**

What views do you see frequently in the popular media about this issue?

> Prompt: To what extent do you agree with these views?

When the historical Buddha ventured outside the palace gates, he discovered that there was great truth and meaning awaiting him. What are our palace gates?

> Prompt: What do we need to learn more about outside our palace gates?

More questions about assumptions and perspectives focused on the broader context:

_____

_____

_____

_____

_____

Understanding Interests and Power Relationships

The questions in this section (Figure 6.3) enable group members to explore and understand whose interests are at the heart of a discussion and how power influences perspectives, decision making, and outcomes. Given the nature of these questions, pay particular attention to your delivery style (body language, tone of voice, inflection) so that your inquiries are as neutral as possible.

Focus: The Individual

Given each member's expertise and supportive organizational resources, who should take responsibility for which tasks?

Think about the leaders in this organization (sector) who have the most influence and positional power. Whom do you identify with the most, and why?

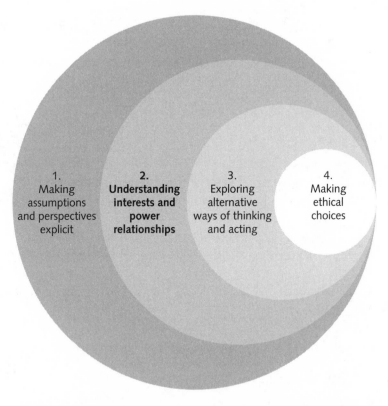

Figure 6.3. Understanding Interests and Power Relationships.

Who has experience in a similar situation with respect to this issue? (*Variation:* Substitute other capacities for *has experience in,* such as "has successfully addressed" or "has studied.")

Who could be taken advantage of in this situation?

> Prompt: Why might this happen?

Who stands to benefit from leaving things the way they are?

> Prompt: Who stands to lose? (*Variations:* "Who stands to benefit from the changes we are considering?" "Who stands to lose?")

In sociopolitical terms, thinking critically entails the habit and ability of asking awkward questions. Questions such as "Why are nearly all faculty at my college white, and nearly all the service staff black or Hispanic?" Questions such as "How can a government condemn other countries' shipments of arms to a nation as wrong, when we're doing the same thing secretly?" . . . Being critically alert also means being able to make connections between personal circumstances (such as the closing of a local health facility, a farm foreclosure, or the appearance of more street people in a town) and broader political happenings (cutting health services budgets, removing farm subsidies, or adopting community mental health policies and consequently reducing residential care for the mentally ill).

—*Brookfield, 1987*

Who will experience a change in profile as a result of participating in or supporting this project?

> Prompt: Describe the expected change and its impact on these individuals.

Whose interests are being served in this situation?

> Prompts: How is this happening? What are the implications?

Whose interests are not being served in this situation?

> Prompts: How is this happening? What are the implications?

More questions about interests and power relationships focused on the individual:

_____

_____

_____

_____

_____

6

Focus: The Team or Organization

Complete these two sentences: Formally and on paper, real power in our organization lies with. . . . Informally and in practice, real power in our organization lies with. . . .

Complete these sentences: If we had . . . involved in this issue then we could make the changes we think are essential. In our organization we make decisions as if. . . . We would function better by making decisions as if. . . .

   Prompt: How can we make our second set of as-ifs a reality?

The more homogeneous our team is, the more focused and perhaps narrower the range of ideas we are likely to generate. How are we homogeneous?"

   Prompts: How are we not? Do we need to make any adjustments to encourage an influx of new ideas? How do we think alike? differently?

To what degree (a lot? a little?) is information a source of power in our organization?

   Prompt: How is information shared or guarded?

> Questions are the best tool you have to help people explore what they don't know.
>
> —Dotlich and Cairo, 1999

What are the first words that come to mind to describe how this group functions?

   Prompt: What made you choose those words? Give specific incidents as examples.

What do people argue about most in our organization?

   Prompt: What is at stake in these arguments?

What key incidents in our history have helped shape how we are organized?

6

What kinds of information do you consider as private in your organization, that is, not to be known outside of the organization?

> Prompt: Why should this information be kept private?

What is one aspect of how we are structured that works well for us? What can we do to ensure that it continues to work well?

> Prompts: What is one aspect of how we are structured that doesn't work well for us? What can we do to improve this aspect?

What is the dominant color that comes to mind when you think about how your group (organization) functions? Why did you choose this color?

> Prompt: What would you like the dominant color to be? Please explain. (*Variations:* Substitute other words and phrases for *color,* "sound," "car," "animal.")

When you hear the phrase *positive use of power,* who comes to mind in your organization?

> **Tip: Ask for specific examples.**

Who has the greatest potential for gain as a result of this crisis (decision, change process)?

> Prompt: Who has the greatest potential for loss as a result of this crisis, decision, or change process?

You are being interviewed off the record and confidentially by a reporter from a business magazine, who asks, "Who is really in charge in your organization?" What do you reply?

More questions about interests and power relationships focused on the team or organization:

_____

_____

_____

_____

_____

_____

Focus: The Broader Context

Consider and respond to this quotation in light of the . . . strike in our province:

> The late Everett Hughes, a pioneering sociologist of the professions, once observed that the professions have struck a bargain with society. In return for access to their extraordinary knowledge in matters of great human importance, society has granted them a mandate for social control in their fields of specialization, a high degree of autonomy in their practice, and a license to determine who shall assume the mantle of professional authority. But in the current climate of criticism, controversy, and dissatisfaction, the bargain is coming unstuck. When the professions' claim to extraordinary knowledge is so much in question, why should we continue to grant them extraordinary rights and privileges? (Schön, 1987, p. 7)

(*Variation:* Use other quotations to prompt critical reflection with group members.)

In your experience, would the failure of this initiative be appealing to any other groups or organizations?

> Prompts: If yes, why might this be so? How might we address this (for example, through constructive dialogue) with those involved?

6

149

Do we ever inadvertently create problems for those with whom we are interdependent?

> Prompts: How does this happen? Why does this happen? What is the impact of this interdependence on our public and customers? How can we prevent this from happening in the future? If this happens in the future, how can we respond in support of our interdependency?

How are decisions made (for example, by consensus, voting, authority) about major issues in our community?

> Prompt: Is there a difference between how high-risk decisions are made and how others are made? Are people comfortable with how this is done?

People often find it difficult to ask for things that they think are important in society. When you think about the issue of . . . in our country today, what would you like to ask your government for?

> Prompts: What are the risks involved in making this request? How could you get others involved in making this request?

What are the benefits (interests) of our organization being a strong leader in this sector?

> Prompts: Are our interests compatible with our organization's national commitment to corporate social responsibility in this sector? What are the costs of our organization being a strong leader in this sector? Are these costs compatible with our financial bottom line?

> **Tip: Avoid a polarized debate on benefits and costs; explore interrelationships instead.**

6

What careful choices do we need to make in relation to community priorities and resources?

> Prompt: What values should guide how we make these choices?

With which organizations are we interdependent?

> Prompts: How are we interdependent? What is the impact of this inter-dependence on us? What is the impact of this interdependence on our publics? Who benefits most from this interdependence? Who does not benefit as a result of this interdependence? Which organizations or groups have special status in our community? How are we held mutually account-able?

More questions about interests and power relationships focused on the broader context:

_____

_____

_____

_____

_____

_____

Exploring Alternative Ways of Thinking and Acting

Facilitators need questions that stimulate participants to be creative when dis-cussing challenges and problems. The next set of questions encourages people to look at options: new ways of approaching old situations, innovative approaches to challenges and dilemmas (Figure 6.4).

Focus: The Individual

A preferred scenario is a detailed, concrete description of a desired state. People are helped to construct preferred scenarios by asking and answering a series of questions such as these:

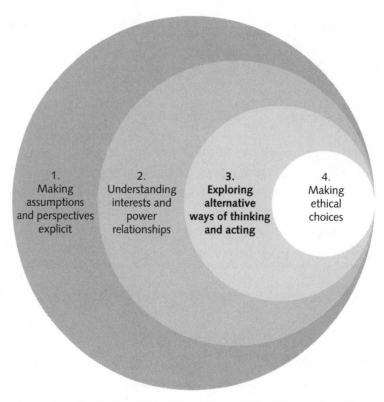

Figure 6.4. Exploring Alternative Ways of Thinking and Acting.

- What would this problem look like if it were managed better?

- What changes would take place in my present lifestyle?

- What would I be doing differently with the people in my life?

- What patterns of behavior would be in place that currently are not?

- What patterns of behavior that are currently in place would be eliminated?

- What would exist that does not exist now?

- What would happen that does not happen now?

- What would I have that I do not have now?

- What decisions would be made and executed?

- What accomplishments would be in place that are not now? (Brookfield, 1987, pp. 120–121)

Describe the ideal workplace for you or someone in your position. Describe it in terms of physical space, location, hours, colleagues, remuneration, benefits, and stress.

If a ten-year-old were asked to address this issue, what would he do?

If you were the president of this company, what would be your first course of action to address this situation?

> Prompt: What would be your second course of action?

If you could have three thoughtful individuals or leaders in your field on this task force, who would they be and why?

> Prompt: What do you think they would suggest as options for action in this situation?

> **Tip: Be sure to check the inferences that will result from the previous question.**

Imagine that it is three years from today and this issue has been completely resolved to your satisfaction. What is going on that is different from today?

Imagine that it is two years from today and I am a reporter from a high-profile magazine in your sector. I have come to interview you about how you have turned around a difficult situation so that others in your situation can benefit from learning about what you have done. What were the biggest problems you were facing two years ago?

> Prompts: What risks were involved in your decision? What is different now from two years ago?

> **Tip: Identify differences in both work and personal life.**

Think of someone whom you consider to be a leader in your organization in the area we are discussing. What do you think her position would be on this issue as it affects your organization?

Think about an important goal that you have achieved in your life. What factors (personal characteristics, support systems, attitudes) helped you achieve that goal?

> Prompt: To what extent could those factors be helpful to you in this situation?

Think of someone in your organization who is skilled at critical thinking. In preparation for our next session, discuss this topic with that person and ask for his insights.

Think about a political decision that has had a significant impact on your life (closing a school, major change in the health care system, decision to have mandatory military service). Describe the impact on your life. Identify the benefits that your government expected from this decision. What was the final result from your perspective, in terms of a cost-benefit analysis?

What are our best intentions with respect to addressing this issue?

What is one thing that needs to happen to make you feel better about your workplace?

What is the first thing you would do to address this situation if tomorrow you became the chair of your organization's board of directors?

> Prompt: How could you achieve the same result over the next few months without becoming chair?

What might be the take of a left-leaning political leader on this situation? and a right-leaning leader?

> Prompt: How would these perspectives compare with your take on the situation?

6

More questions about alternative ways of thinking and acting focused on the individual:

_____

_____

_____

_____

_____

_____

Focus: The Team or Organization

Draw a horizontal line that everyone can see. At the far right end, write "most expensive" and at the far left end write "least expensive." Ask, "What are all the alternative actions you can think of that would fit on this continuum?" (*Variation:* Ask participants to complete continua for a number of extremes, such as riskiest to least risky.)

Given the benefits and risks involved, when might be the best time for us to act?

Have our organizational values shifted over the past five years? If yes, how and why?

How does this approach fit with your organization's culture—the way things are done?

How have we done this in the past? What did we learn that could help us now?

Let's check this draft list of strategic priorities against our company mission. Do they fit well, or do we need to make some adjustments?

Think about the current situation we are discussing. What are all the possible approaches that you suspect organizational change experts might recommend?

> Prompt: Problem solvers sometimes create a new tool or "hammer" and then see lots of situations as potential "nails." Which of these approaches might be a legitimate "hammer" for our unique situation?

What are the potential consequences for your organization of doing nothing about the current situation?"

6

155

Prompt: What are the potential consequences of making a decision to . . . ?

What are the risks (potential harmful consequences) for our organization in each of the suggested alternatives?

What do you feel good about with respect to how your organization has responded to the current situation?

Prompts: What do you feel disappointed about with respect to how your organization has responded to the current situation? What alternative approaches come to mind?

When you consider our current market penetration, what is our preferred scenario for one year from today?

Whom could you count on for support if you made some significant changes in how this group functions?

More questions about alternative ways of thinking and acting focused on the organization:

_____

_____

_____

_____

_____

_____

Focus: The Broader Context

Consider this quotation: "The right of the individual is the power that upholds the right of the community, just as, conversely, it is the community that upholds and defends the rights of the individual" (Bonhoeffer, 1993, p. 173). How do we as individuals support our community?

Prompt: How do we as a community support the rights of individuals in our larger community?

How do other cultures approach this issue? (*Variation:* Replace *cultures* with "countries.")

Think of a situation in your province or state where the division between the haves and the have-nots is significant in relation to the issue being discussed. Then:

- Brainstorm all the possible solutions you can think of.

- Consider the risks and benefits of your preferred approach before confirming that it is a wise choice.

- Develop a list of conditions (outcomes) to describe a successful solution to this situation.

- Play your optional solutions against the list of conditions and choose a possible approach.

- What perspectives are there on what to do about the situation?

- Why does this situation exist?

What other groups (companies, organizations, countries) have been faced with this situation? What did they do?

> Prompts: How was their context similar to or different from ours? What happened as a result of their actions? What implications does their experience have for us?

Where else have you seen this approach work?

> Prompt: What key features make it work in that setting?

More questions about alternative ways of thinking and acting focused on the broader context:

_____

_____

_____

_____

_____

6

Today it's not just a matter of deciding right from wrong. Often as not, we have to decide between right and right, and wrong and wrong. In our times, as Camus said, we are clear that the cry for clean hands that might come from making exactly "right" decisions is the cry of a damned soul. There are no clean hands. For many people who appreciate their own degree of moral probity this is painful. The fact is that our time uses a different metaphor and a different set of principles. In many situations we have to deal with, there are no rules. We have only our critical intelligence to determine what is really needed. Today, we ask not what is right, but what is responsible. Not what is good or bad, but what is befitting or appropriate. Not whether it is honest or pure, but whether it is necessary and responsible.

—*Stanfield, 2000b*

Making Ethical Choices

Individuals make ethical choices when they are clear about their values and how they act on them (their ethical standards). Organizations make ethical choices and function better if the people involved are clear about what their values are and how they act on them.

Facilitators can encourage participants to think about ethics in many ways and situations: to understand a point of view, explore an ethical dilemma, raise awareness about potential wrongdoing, consider the impact of a decision on other stakeholders, or explore issues related to power. The next set of questions (suggested by Figure 6.5) encourage participants to consider how to make right choices leading to ethical action that is based on their values.

Focus: The Individual

Think about yourself when you were a new employee coming into this company.
   How did you want to be treated?

   Prompt: Is this how we treat the people we supervise now?

To what extent do you agree or disagree with the statement, "How we work in our organization reflects the personal philosophy of our president"? Please

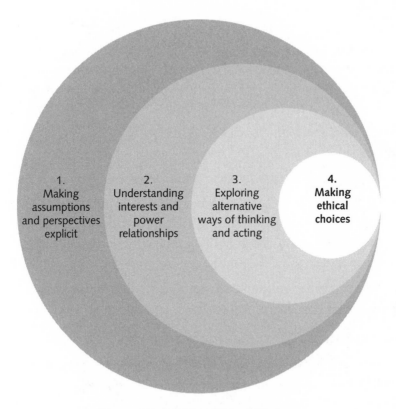

1.
Making
assumptions
and perspectives
explicit

2.
Understanding
interests and
power
relationships

3.
Exploring
alternative
ways of thinking
and acting

4.
Making
ethical
choices

Figure 6.5. Making Ethical Choices.

explain, using specific examples. (*Variation:* Substitute other words or phrases for *president,* perhaps "senior management" or "employee assistance program.")

Tip: To frame this response, use a scale of 1 as low to 4 as high so that participants must make a clear choice that leans toward one end of the scale or another, not a noncommittal response of 3 on a scale of 1 to 5.

The values of the individual employee are intrinsic to the achievement of our business objectives.

—*A manager/facilitator*

> *The golden rule: Do unto others as you would like them to do unto you.*

What are the values that underlie this point of view?

What kind of ethical dilemma does this initiative present for you?

How did your parents express their expectations about ethical behavior to you? Give an example of an expectation.

How is the current situation consistent (or inconsistent) with your values?

Imagine that it is New Year's Eve and you are sitting down with the president and vice president of your board of directors to make corporate resolutions for the year to come. What is one corporate value you would encourage these two leaders to act on over the coming year?

Think about someone you admire in your organization (group). What do you admire about how that person acts?

> Prompts: What is the value that underlies such behavior? How do you act (or not act) on that value in your life? What could you do more of (or less of) to enhance how you implement that value in your life?

Think of an incident that makes you feel good about your organization. What is it about this incident that makes you feel good?

> Prompt: What is the value that is at play in this incident?

6

What is one rule you grew up with that you think is important for raising children today?

> Prompt: What is one rule you grew up with that you would not use with your children today?

> The toughest ethical issues have no right or wrong, no black or white, but shades of gray. Every choice has costs. This is the definition of an ethical dilemma. Not only is there no right or wrong, but coaches in good conscience differ about which is the lesser evil.
>
> —Clark, 1994

What is our intention here? Are we comfortable with this intention?

What is one thing you learned previously that has helped to shape your views on this issue?

What would push you to make a radical change in your lifestyle? Think of something significant—for example, something that affects how you support yourself, or with whom you spend time, or how you act on your beliefs.

Who are the most important people in your life?

> Prompts: How do they contribute to your life? How do you contribute to their lives?

More questions about making ethical choices focused on the individual:

_____

_____

_____

_____

_____

_____

Focus: The Team or Organization

A rights-based approach to organizational change emphasizes understanding and realizing human rights for all. Human rights include the right to life, a basic education, privacy, and equality before the law, as well as the rights to vote and be elected, work, and attain a high standard of physical and mental health. Are you aware of our organization denying any employees' human rights?

Describe a critical incident that occurred within the last six months and that demonstrates how senior managers act on organizational values. Name the value in question.

> **Tip: Ask participants to choose an incident that stands out for them, whether positive or negative in relation to organizational values.**

6

How do our board of directors and chief executive officer signal their ethical expectations? (Dalla Costa, 1998, p. 258)

> Prompts: How is senior management accountable for ethical performance? How are shareholders engaged in issues and decisions regarding ethical performance?

> When business logic asks, Where is the advantage? ethical logic asks, How does this decision affect the dignity of others? Over time, this question evolves into a combined and interactive one: What business advantage of human dignity toward customers, employees, partners, suppliers and the community adds to competitive advantage?
>
> —Dalla Costa, 1998

How do you encourage the national office employees in your labor union to engage in critical thinking for the benefit of members?

How does our organization support the health of employees through its human resource policies?

How does this organization express its expectations about ethical behavior to employees and board members? Give an example of an expectation.

How fair are our charity's practices with respect to donors, employees, stakeholders, and the public?

Looking forward, what do you see as a best scenario?

> Prompt: Looking backward, what have we learned that will help us achieve that best scenario?

Think about how this group works together. In what areas are you most comfortable being candid with one another?

> Prompts: In what areas are you least comfortable? How could you expand the degree of candor in the group?

Think of your organization as a growing person. How mature is it? Is it a newborn, a young child, an adolescent, a young adult, a mature adult, or an older person? Explain your response with specific examples.

6

What are the three most important values you hold as a board member for this charity?

> Prompt: From your perspective, how operational are these values in how this organization conducts its business?

What criteria should guide how we make decisions during this process?

What is your organization's greatest achievement?

> Prompt: How do you contribute to that achievement?

What two or three words would you like people to associate with your organization?

What values does your organization espouse (formally through a strategic plan, or informally through leadership)?

> Prompt: If you could change one thing that would ensure your organization was more ethical, what would it be?

What would a rights approach to this issue look like in our organization?

> Prompt: How will we know that we have made the right decisions?

Whom will this decision affect?

> Prompts: How will it affect them? How comfortable would you be if you had to live with the impact of this decision?

Whom are you responsible for (obligated to) when you make this decision?

> Prompt: How are you reflecting this responsibility in how you make this decision?

You have been assigned as mentor to a new employee (board member, group member) who will be taking your place as you move to a new position. This person has asked you what he should do to build positive working relationships with subordinates. What would you tell him?

More questions about making ethical choices focused on the organization:

_____

_____

_____

_____

_____

_____

Focus: The Broader Context

> Just as individual ethics can only be understood in relation to the society within which it is practiced, it is also true that individual ethical behavior is far likelier to flourish within a just society. Indeed, it might be argued that to lead an ethical life one must work to build a just society.
>
> —*Cohen, 2002*

How does our organization participate in global ethical (or social justice) issues related to our industry?

How does our organization support the health of the community in which we are located?

Rights-based approaches to political and economic issues around the globe are attaining a higher profile and sometimes supplanting needs approaches. What meaning could this statement have for our organization with respect to the issues we are discussing?

What do you think are the top most important values for parents to teach their children in our society?

Prompt: To what extent are these values operational in your current community or work situation?

What injustices are you aware of in your community that you would like to see addressed?

Prompts: How could your organization play a useful role in addressing these injustices? Who in your organization could take the lead in this area?

What is our organization's reputation when it comes to ethical issues or doing the right thing?

More questions about making ethical choices focused on the broader context:

_____

_____

_____

_____

_____

_____

COMMON CHALLENGES

These real-life examples explore opportunities for conscious use of questions in a number of common situations.

Thinking Critically About the Future

Challenge: We are a well-known national environmental agency. We are under pressure from our members and funders as well as interested politicians and advocacy groups to rethink our position on global warming. Recent international environmental agreements are also putting a spotlight on our work. We are having a one-day meeting of our board of directors at which we want to spend time reflecting on our current situation and thinking about our future.

What questions can you suggest to frame this agenda?

Response: Use the process framework in this chapter to help set up the main parts of your agenda. Here are sample reflective questions.

Assumptions and Perspectives

Our current policy on global warming states that. . . . What assumptions underlie this policy?

What do we know now that we didn't know when we developed this policy about global warming?

6

Interests and Power Relationships

Who stands to gain the most from our current policy on global warming?

Who stands to lose the most from our current policy on global warming?

Alternative Approaches

What is our preferred scenario for global warming ten years from today?

How do our current policies potentially support or block that preferred scenario?

Ethical Choices

What ethical choices do we need to make in relation to our current policies on warming?

How might our organizational mission and values help us in making these choices?

Acting Ethically in Low-Resource Countries

Challenge: The textile group in our multinational corporation was experiencing a lot of pressure from a range of groups and organizations regarding how we were paying our workers in low-resource countries. As the vice president of human resources, I asked a reputable consulting company with links to another country's well-known international development program to (1) review our policies and practices, (2) provide a report to our senior leadership group (twelve people) on whether or not we were behaving ethically in these countries, and (3) facilitate a one-day process focused on corporate social responsibility and ethical behavior in relation to the report results.

Response: The leadership group carried out a review of the report based on the questions appearing here. Their conclusions were then used to create a special task force to address outstanding issues.

When the group reported to us, they cautioned that "everybody wants a box of chocolates and a long-stemmed rose" (Leonard Cohen, "Everybody Knows") and that this would not be happening with this report, even though the report had some complimentary things to say about how we were functioning abroad.

166

Before the report was handed out, we were asked, "As senior leaders in this organization who have visited the overseas plants that have recently been reviewed, what is your best guess about the top three conclusions in this report?" Our responses were summarized in plenary. Then we were given two hours to review the report and make notes on these questions:

Overall, how comfortable are you with this report? Please explain.

Given the mission and values of our group, how are we behaving ethically in our overseas locations? How are we behaving unethically?

In plenary discussion, we summarized our responses to the questions and then discussed the current situation in terms of win-lose scenarios: Who is winning, and who is losing? in which ways? What are the possibilities of creating a win-win situation in each country?

The session closed with two final questions:

What is revealed by comparison of what we thought the report would say and what it actually said about our leadership in other countries?

What are the key questions about our corporate ethics that we need to ask ourselves in the future?

In a later debriefing session, participants in this process remarked that it was one of the most stimulating days they had experienced during their tenure with our company. They expressed surprise that although no decisions were taken and there was very little focus on action, the change in perspective was significant and would result in new ways of doing things that were not part of their awareness prior to the session.

6

Thinking Critically About Policy Changes

Challenge: We are moving our government's support for physical fitness programs and classes to a broader approach called Active Living. What can we do to help our policy group think critically about this transition and how our new policy on Active Living will differ from how we have worked in the past under a narrower physical fitness approach?

Response: Use this bank of questions as a starting point for the policy group to think critically about Active Living and thus deepen their understanding of the concept. Group members can select questions from the list to frame their discussion.

The Basics

Are there minimum standards for Active Living?

How can we describe Active Living?

> Prompts: Why this term? Whom is it for? How is it unique? What is the role of physical activity in Active Living?

How do we know that living actively enhances well-being?

How does the notion of personal empowerment fit with the concept of Active Living?

Is Active Living a measurable concept?

> Prompts: If so, how do you measure it? If not, what are the implications of driving a concept that can't be measured?

Is Active Living a new fad?

Is there a typical prescription for Active Living?

> Prompt: If so, can you describe it?

How do we address exercise intensity through Active Living?

What are some examples of Active Living?

What do we (the government) want to achieve with Active Living?

What does the concept of Active Living include?

> Prompts: Does it go beyond being active physically and include being active as a community leader? Are there any guidelines for defining Active Living?

6

Links to Other Areas

Does Active Living include work-related physical activity as well as leisure-time physical activity?

How can physical activity be an important feature of activities that are essentially mental, social, or spiritual?

Is Active Living supported by existing social norms and values?

What is the relationship between Active Living and the environment? (*Variations:* Replace *the environment* with "health," "recreation and leisure," "sport," "the workplace.")

Active Living and Fitness

Does Active Living include performance goals?

Does cardiovascular fitness remain an important issue?

Has the definition of physical activity changed?

Is Active Living just fitness with the name changed?

When fitness was the goal, individuals knew whether they were fit. How do people know if they are living actively?

The Department's Role

How do we manage this change process?

How does Active Living fit with our department's current Blueprints for Action?

What are the implications of Active Living for existing departmental policies, programs, activities, and organizational structures?

What could Active Living look like over the next two years?

What is the difference between Active Living and our department's current health promotion initiatives?

What is the process for incorporating Active Living into our department's current activities?

Will Active Living be a new program in our department?

6

Implementation

If freedom of choice and individual fit are inherent in the concept, does it mean that each individual should have access to a full range of opportunities?

Should we continue to encourage Canadians to move along a continuum from minimum-level physical activity to more intense, regular physical activity?

Leadership

How will group fitness leaders be involved in Active Living initiatives?

If Active Living focuses on the individual, who is responsible at the group level for Active Living?

What is the best role for our department with respect to Active Living?

Will Active Living result in an enlarged mandate for our department?

Programs

Does implementing Active Living require additional resources (time, money, knowledge, equipment, space, social organization)?

If the concept of Active Living suggests that individuals can incorporate any type of physical activity (such as walking) into their daily lives, is there still a need for structured programs?

Promotion and Communication

What are our policies for communicating Active Living to other government departments? (*Variations:* Substitute "health-related organizations" or "the public in general" for *government departments.*)

What is the difference between promoting participation in physical activity in accordance with a fitness concept and doing so in accordance with the Active Living concept?

6

7 Questions for Addressing Issues

Understanding and addressing issues is often a central part of facilitated processes, as with strategic planning, team development, network building, advocacy, policy development, and general problem solving.

PROCESS FRAMEWORK

Focused and systematic questioning enables people to have the meaningful conversations required to address issues collectively. The process framework in this chapter enables facilitators to support groups in addressing six main challenges when discussing issues (Figure 7.1).

Although (as mentioned in the Preface) the questions in this chapter are designed for verbal interaction during a session, they can also be adapted for written feedback forms.

Although at first glance it may look as if these six areas are sequential steps, how you approach an issue and related challenges depends on the situation. We often identify key issues with a planning committee and then develop a concise statement (a single sentence) describing the challenge for each issue. Then the next items follow as listed in the figure, or if others have already completed some of them we review their work to understand it better and then complete the outstanding steps.

As with every chapter in this book, it is essential to customize both the process framework and the questions to suit your situation. This framework is flexible and

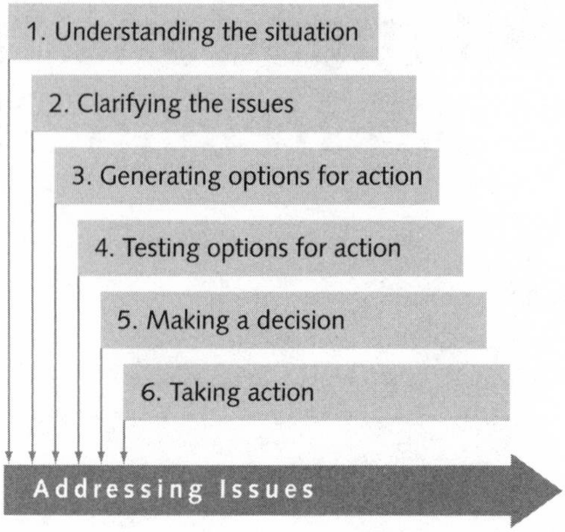

Figure 7.1. Process Framework for Addressing Issues.

designed to accommodate a range of approaches and tools that individual organizations may have developed or that are part of a facilitators toolkit, such as SWOT analysis (strengths, weaknesses, opportunities, threats) or PEST (political, economic, sociocultural, and technological factors; www.marketingteacher.com/Lessons).

GUIDELINES FOR QUESTIONS TO ADDRESS ISSUES

Questions for addressing issues usually fit within the context of a larger process. For example, in strategic planning they may guide development of goals; in team development they may help to identify and understand team-building challenges.

The guidelines given here support effective use of questions in addressing issues.

- Clarify terminology, customizing a glossary to suit your situation (for instance, "For the purposes of this process, here is what we mean by the following terms:

- Issue: an important topic for debate, dialogue, and discussion, often involving tension, challenges, and specific problems; issues are a normal part of organizational life.

- Challenge: a demanding or difficult task or situation that tests people's abilities; clarifying challenges is an important initial step in addressing an issue.

- Challenge statement: a single sentence that begins with "The challenge in this priority is to. . . ."

- Problem: something to be solved, an obstacle or barrier that has a potential solution; usually part of a larger issue.

- Mystery: a problem that eludes typical problem solving.

- Think of problems as friends. Problems are inevitable, and you can't learn or be successful without them. Too often, change-related problems are ignored, denied, or treated as an occasion for blame and defense. Successful change efforts are more likely when problems are treated as natural, expected phenomena with their own unique tensions and confusion. The way to deal with these realities is not to cover them up, but to ask the types of questions that lead to enhanced understanding and action.

> Life doesn't follow straight-line logic; it conforms to a kind of curved logic that changes the nature of things and often turns them into their opposites. Problems, then, are not just hassles to be dealt with and set aside. Lurking inside each problem is a workshop on the nature of organizations and a vehicle for personal growth. This entails a shift; we need to value the process of finding the solution—juggling the inconsistencies that meaningful solutions entail.
>
> —Pascale, 1990

7

- Encourage participants to go to where the tension is in a particular topic or during a discussion ("I'm getting the feeling that a particularly sensitive topic is at the heart of this issue"). If participants agree then ask, "Where does all the tension come from?"

• Confirm that your role as facilitator is to be aware of and primarily neutral about content while functioning as a process expert. Be clear about the implications of this stance: your focus is on avoiding conflict of interest and ensuring a high-quality decision-making process, not influencing outcomes (see Chapter Two).

• Take a comprehensive approach to the context of an issue. For facilitators, this means that background information for discussing an issue must be inclusive and representative of a variety of perspectives and orientations. Inclusiveness up front encourages ownership for a solution developed later on.

• Explore the terrain. Encourage participants to consider a variety of perspectives on an issue ("Does everyone have the same understanding of this situation? What other perspectives are in this group?")

• Limit the number of issues that can be addressed given the time available. Don't crowd your agenda or overwork the group; protect enough discussion time to ensure that participants build ownership for both their understanding of the issue and how they can contribute to its resolution.

• Use lateral-thinking techniques and processes (brainstorming, mind mapping, open space) to encourage divergent thinking about issues and their solutions.

• As you summarize participants' input in a written report, make your document specific, straightforward, and as brief as possible so that participants can get to the main points quickly (such as strengths and weaknesses). Avoid complex dis-

1. Creative thinkers reject standardized formats for problem solving.

2. They have interests in a wide range of related and divergent fields.

3. They can take multiple perspectives on a problem.

4. They view the world as relative and contextual rather than universal and absolute.

5. They frequently use trial-and-error methods in their experimentation with alternative approaches.

6. They have a future orientation; change is embraced optimistically as a valuable developmental possibility.

7. They have self-confidence and trust in their own judgment.

—Brookfield, 1987

cussion and overanalysis so that those working with the report are comfortable using it during group discussion.

• Ensure that the solution takes into account the potential impact on the whole system rather than on only one part of it (Senge, 1990; Scholtes, 1998; Stanfield, 2000b).

• Avoid any question that is actually an indirect statement about an issue ("How did such a negative spin get put on this problem?").

• When it comes to participants, it's "quality in, quality out" ("How will you ensure that you have the right people in the room to get the best possible product from your process investment?")

• If a discussion about issues is turning too abstract and conceptual, ask specific questions that focus participants on a particular aspect or action step that is practical in nature.

• Offer a clear and well-organized outline for how the issue will be explored. This clarity supports participants' comfort with and confidence in the process.

• Describe how decisions will be made and confirm the approach with participants. Explain clearly linkages among the overall process, how decisions will be made, and expectations about participant engagement in implementation. If participants are uncomfortable with how decisions are made, they are less likely to support implementation.

• Clarify the scope of the issue, confirming that those engaged in the process are comfortable with the boundaries for discussion and decision making. Be absolutely clear about what is on and off the table in terms of the issue. You may want to include a discussion about boundaries in setting group norms.

QUESTION BANK

The question bank for this chapter focuses on the six main areas in the process framework for addressing issues (Figure 7.1). Subsections in each area help to focus your questioning. It is important to customize individual questions, paying attention to nuance and to how you have adapted the process framework to fit your situation. The questions in this bank are useful for a range of facilitation technologies, among them force field analysis, SWOT analysis, sequential questioning, and gap analysis (Bens, 2000).

7

Understanding the Situation

Questions that work hard to address issues result in the information needed to get a comprehensive picture of a situation (Figure 7.2). These questions solicit participants' views on topics such as how a team is functioning, working relationships within an organization or group, the status of previous initiatives, and the general environment in which the organization is functioning.

Focus: Internal Considerations

Are there any areas of our business where staff commitment might be a concern?

> Prompt: If yes, why is that?

Are there any underlying issues in our organization that might affect how well we work together?

As a partner in this firm, what do you think are the three most important things you spend time doing?

> Tip: Ask other participants for their perspectives on what are the most important things that partners in the firm do.

As a senior manager, what keeps you awake at night when you think about the future of our organization?

At last year's retreat you set an action plan to address three priorities: . . . As the report for this retreat indicates, you are satisfied with what you accomplished for two of these areas and dissatisfied with the third. Which aspects of last year's plan should be carried over to our discussion this year?

What words would you use to describe the spirit that people in our organization bring to the problems and tensions associated with change-related issues: open? closed? inquiry? apathy? solutions? others?

> Prompt: How do we know this?

From your perspective, what signs and symptoms indicate challenges that need addressing?

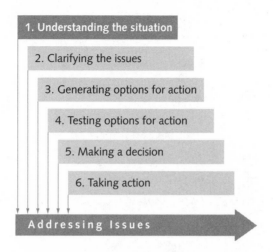

Figure 7.2. Understanding the Situation.

Given our resources, what is one thing we could do to improve how we work together?

How do you know when you have been successful? unsuccessful?

> Prompt: How do you know when you have been unsuccessful?

If you were in charge, what would be your top two priorities for change over the next two years to ensure a positive future for our organization?

If you could do one thing to improve how we work together as a team, what would it be?

Is there anything about how our organization functions that you find confusing? (*Variation:* Substitute other words and phrases for *confusing*: "surprising," "gratifying," "interesting," "supportive," "unsupportive.")

There are two kinds of issues: the ones we talk about and the ones we don't. Which issues do we talk about?

> Prompt: Which issues do we not talk about?

7

Think about your work group over the past year. Has anything changed significantly about how people work together?

Think about how we do business in relation to this account. What are we good at?

> Prompt: Where could we be better?

To what extent might resources have an impact on strategies we can develop to address this issue?

We have been highly successful in the past at. . . . How could our skill and experience in this area contribute to success in addressing this issue?

What are the advantages of being a member of this team? (*Variation:* Substitute "disadvantages" for *advantages.*)

What do people in our internal community say are our strengths and weaknesses?

With respect to the issue, what expectations do you have of others in the organization that are being met to your satisfaction?

> Prompt: What expectations do you have of others that are not being met to your satisfaction?

> Further prompts: What expectations do others have of you that you enjoy meeting? What expectations do others have of you that you prefer not to meet?

What is going well in our community? What do we need to improve?

What pleases you about this organization?

> Prompt: What upsets you about it?

What strengths do we have that could open up opportunities for our consideration?

> Prompt: What weaknesses do we have that, if addressed, would open up additional opportunities?

What would you need to do to significantly enhance how your organization functions?

Where are we most successful and productive as an organization?

> Prompt: Where are we least successful and productive?

Where do we agree as a management team on strategic directions?

> Prompt: Where do we disagree?

Who are not currently your customers but could be?

What do you find satisfying about addressing issues?

> Prompt: What frustrates you about addressing issues?

What do you like most about being a member of this group?

> Prompt: What do you like least?

What is the current trend line for our company's area of expertise?

What is one thing you think your deputy minister (chief executive officer, director, president) should know about the current situation?

What issues are important to people with lesser status and power in our organization?

> Prompt: When will these issues be included in the discussion?

Which key individuals can we count on for support on issues?

> Prompt: What types of support could they provide?

More questions on internal considerations:

_____

_____

_____

_____

_____

7

Focus: External Considerations

Does the current economy support what we want to do? (*Variation:* Replace *current* with "near future" or "distant future.")

From your perspective, what opportunities are emerging as a result of changes in the environment within which our firm operates?

> Prompt: What threats are emerging?

> **Tip: Provide key words to generate ideas, such as *political, environmental, economic, genetic, demographic, sociocultural, technological.***

How does the public view your organization?

> Prompt: What evidence do you have of these views?

How do we compare in terms of . . . to other organizations similar to us in purpose and size?

If we were to close our doors tomorrow, who would miss us?

> Prompt: Why would they miss us? Who would not miss us that we wish would miss us? Why wouldn't they miss us?

What are our organization's strongest points when it comes to customer satisfaction?

> Prompt: What are our weakest points?

What are the broadest boundaries you can think of for us with respect to this issue?

> Prompt: What boundaries are realistic for us in terms of next steps?

What are the major external threats facing our organization over the next six months?

Prompt: How prepared are we to address these threats?

Further prompts: What key opportunities are on the horizon for us over the next six months? How prepared are we to capitalize on them?

What are the top two or three opportunities that we should be acting on over the next three years to be successful in terms of revenue?

Prompt: What are the top two or three barriers?

Further prompts: What are the strengths of the team in acting on these opportunities and barriers? What are the weaknesses?

What changes are taking place in our milieu that could affect our success in addressing this issue?

What do people in our external community or marketplace say about opportunities and threats with respect to our services or products?

What do our customers say about our service?

What do our press clippings say about us?

What do we know about how well our society accommodates the needs of its . . . ? *Variations:* Insert names of vulnerable groups that are related to your issue: cultural minorities, elderly citizens, people with disabilities, and so forth.

What have you heard or read about lately that rings a bell with respect to this initiative? Think out of the box here—there are no silly answers.

Prompt: When you think about all the ideas we have generated in response to this question, do you see any themes or common ideas?

What factors in the current environment are having an impact on the ability of this task force to do its work?

What forces for change are acting on your organization now?

Prompts: What forces for stability are also present? What challenges does this situation present you for the future?

What interesting trends are you aware of that could have an impact on how we look at this issue?

What is happening globally in relation to our organization's interests that we need to take into account for this initiative? (*Variation:* Replace *globally* with "locally," "in our province or state," "nationally," and so on.)

What situations, initiatives, other networks, and the like offer opportunities for further strengthening our work?

Who are your biggest critics and supporters?

> Prompts: What are they saying? What can you learn from this?

Who or what represents state-of-the-art understanding of this issue?

> Prompt: How can we access their wisdom for our discussion?

> **Tip: Search the Web for references, papers, and so on.**

More questions on external considerations:

_____

_____

_____

_____

_____

_____

Clarifying the Issues

In some situations, the issues are clear and described succinctly through other processes. In most situations, however, it is important to explore perspectives carefully to ensure that there is agreement on what needs to be discussed. In addition, more often than not, what one person or group sees as the issue another person or group interprets as a symptom of a deeper or more complex problem.

Until there is a basic and agreed common understanding of an issue, it is difficult to move forward to explore options for action (Figure 7.3).

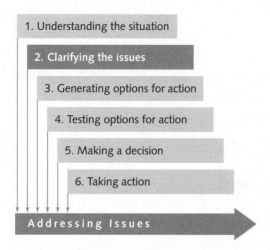

Figure 7.3. Clarifying the Issues.

Focus: Issue Description

Are there any recurring patterns you can see with respect to this issue?

 Prompt: What can we learn from discussing these patterns?

Are we looking at the whole, comprehensive picture, or do we have just one small part of the big picture?

 Prompt: How will we know that we have a comprehensive view?

Can we describe fully what is happening with respect to this issue?

 Prompt: What is the impact of this issue on our group? (*Variations:* Substitute other words for *group,* such as "team," "organization," "jurisdiction," "clients." Substitute various timelines, such as "current impact" or "potential impact.")

Describe the issue as a challenge in a single sentence. For example, "The challenge is to . . ." or "The real issue is . . ." or "Our priority is to. . . ."

Do we have the background information we need to describe and address this problem?

>   **Tip: Avoid an endless hunt for information, which can morph into an avoidance strategy.**

How does this challenge affect your strategic plan (mission, vision, values, strategic directions, priorities, goals)?

>   Prompt: Are changes required?

What broader issues such as human rights, workplace safety, training, and development are tied into these concerns?

What feedback have we received from our customers recently—letters of satisfaction and support, complaints, comments about service, and so on—that may help us understand this problem better?

What is your personal view on this issue?

>   Prompts: What is your view based on? What other personal interests are present? What might they be based on?

What makes this issue complex for our organization? (*Variations:* Substitute other words for *complex*, such as "straightforward," "interesting," "a challenge," "urgent.")

What does a systems perspective of this issue look like?

What specific problems are part of this issue?

What turning points (key events) have we experienced over the past year in relation to this issue?

What aspects of this issue are beyond our control? (*Variation:* "What can't we change about this issue?")

>   **Tip: Review responses in terms of hidden assumptions or biases.**

Where is the silver lining in all this?

More questions on describing the issue:

_____

_____

_____

_____

_____

_____

Focus: Why This Is an Issue

Do you think this issue will become more or less important over the next few years?

> Prompt: Please explain.

How are these issues related to what our organization stands for?

How do you feel about addressing this issue at this time?

How does this issue disrupt things in our community (organization, group)?

How long have you held this view on this issue?

> Prompt: What is happening to reinforce or weaken your point of view?

If you were selecting a product like ours for your home, who would be our competition?

> Prompt: What might encourage you to select a competitor's product?

What are the benefits of getting this issue resolved this year?

> Prompt: What will happen if nothing is done to address this issue?

What are the top three factors that contribute to making this a problem for us?

> Prompts: When did this issue emerge? What helped it develop? How did we respond? Whom did we consult? What have we learned so far?

7

What assumptions about this issue underlie our thinking?

> Prompt: How do, or how could, these assumptions affect our ability to address this issue?

What data or evidence do you have that will help you understand these challenges?

What emotions or heightened feelings are connected with this issue?

> Prompt: What is their source?

What incentives are there to solve this problem?

> Prompt: Are there any incentives for not addressing this problem? (*Variation:* Substitute "perceived benefits" for *incentives.*)

What is going on now that is affecting our customer satisfaction ratings?

> Prompts: How are they being affected? Who are our customers? What do we know about them? What features of our products are most important to our customers?

What is it about this issue that you may be ignoring at your peril?

Is there anything about this issue that is not being said and needs to be heard?

> Prompt: How can we listen to these silences?

What is the history behind this issue in our organization?

What pressures are there for us to address this issue?

Where is our greatest vulnerability in relation to this issue?

> **Tip: When a problem occurs, ask why. Ask why as many times as it takes until you get at the systemic cause of the problem (Scholtes, 1998).**

More questions on why this is an issue:

_____

_____

_____

_____

_____

_____

Focus: Stakeholders

For the best result, we need everyone's wisdom and perspective at our table. Who else needs to be brought on board? Whose views are we missing?

For whom is this an issue? How is it an issue?

> **Tip: Chapter Six has a number of questions that are also effective for analyzing issues.**

How do the politics in our organization have an impact on this issue?

How does this issue affect you?

> Prompts: How does it affect you personally? in terms of your job? your family life? Is there a specific problem that concerns you the most?

How inclusive are we in our approach to understanding this issue?

> Prompt: Whose perspective is not being taken into consideration?

How might . . . see our role in addressing this issue?

In what other settings or circumstances have you encountered a similar issue?

> Prompts: How was it handled? What did you notice or learn that could be helpful to this situation?

What employee cultures are involved in this issue? Are you including their perspectives in trying to understand this issue?

What is unique about this issue or problem?

Which parts of our organization are most affected by this issue?

> Prompts: Which are least affected? Why do you think things happened this way?

Who are our internal cheerleaders on this issue?

> Prompt: Who are our external cheerleaders?

Who else (other than your team members) is connected to this issue (problem)?

> Prompt: How can they influence the outcome?

Who has a stake in this issue?

> Prompt: What is it?

Who is responsible in our formal and informal organizational structures for providing leadership in addressing this problem?

Who will or can influence what decisions we make? Who is likely to be affected by decisions we need to make?

> Prompts: How can we get these perspectives to the table? What do we need to do (if anything) to accommodate those who can influence or be affected by our decisions?

More questions on stakeholders:

_____

_____

_____

_____

_____

_____

7

Generating Options for Action

Questions that enable people to visualize a positive future with respect to an issue can establish a strong basis for developing options for action (Figure 7.4). Considering sources of and potential solutions for an issue and learning about what others have done in similar situations also contributes to a focus on next steps.

Focus: A Positive Future

Imagine that you are being interviewed two years from today by a reporter from a prestigious journal. He wants to know how your team managed to turn this issue around so successfully. His first question is, "So, what is different today in comparison to two years ago?"

Imagine that it's two years from today and your customers are delighted with your services. What is going on that is different from today? (*Variation:* Substitute other words for *services,* such as "products.")

Think about a positive future that is a realistic stretch for your team. What do you see going on?

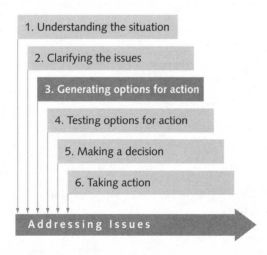

Figure 7.4. Generating Options for Action.

Tip: A realistic stretch encourages participants to think big and dream a little about suggestions that will push their boundaries and venture outside the box but that are still doable. This prevents outrageous responses that no one believes have a chance of working.

Think big—revolution, not evolution. What radical change could we make that would enable us to address this issue successfully?

Prompt: Think "reasonable" —evolution, not revolution. What small change could we make that would have a significant positive impact on this issue?

What are the first words or phrases that come to mind to describe what we're like when we are at the top of our game?

What is our unique contribution to our community over the long run?

What is the one thing we can do now that will have the biggest possible impact on our success over the coming year?

More questions on a positive future:

_____

_____

_____

_____

_____

_____

Focus: Solutions

If you had the power and capacity to do something unique in this situation, what would it be?

In what ways are we stuck?

Prompt: What do we need to do to get unstuck and address this issue successfully?

What are our criteria for effective solutions?

> Tip: Work with a small, representative group to create a draft set of criteria for use with this question. Keep the list small; five or six are usually enough.

What are the most obvious solutions to this problem?

> Prompt: What are less obvious solutions?

What do you hear people complaining about most in relation to this issue?

> Prompts: What could we do immediately to address some of these complaints? What could we do over the long run?

What factors in our organization (such as systems and policies) enable this problem to continue?

What is a relatively small problem that you can fix now that will have a major positive impact on your customers?

What is going on now with respect to this issue that should not be happening?

> Prompt: What should be going on now that is not?

What opportunities does this issue present us with?

What options can we generate that take a whole-system perspective?

What potential solutions would be most relevant to our customers? (*Variations:* Replace *our customers* with " our professional community," "our employees," "our shareholders," "our board members," or " our advocates.")

What would it take to deal with this issue?

Thinking in polarities reduces both our creativity and our options. What are some polarity traps (opposites) we could get into with respect to this issue— that is, "Either we do this or we do that"?

> Prompt: How can we break out of this type of thinking?

What is one thing we know for sure about the bottom line here?

7

More questions on sources and solutions:

_____

_____

_____

_____

_____

_____

Focus: Learning from Others

In many situations involving complex, long-standing issues, there are a few people who are keen about trying new approaches. Who might these people be in your situation?

> Prompt: What are their perspectives?

What does the literature on best practices in . . . say about addressing issues like this one?

What innovative approaches to this problem have you seen, heard about, or wanted to explore?

What would someone with nothing to lose do in this situation? (*Variations:* Substitute various designations for *someone with nothing to lose,* such as "our retired CEO," or "Peter Drucker.")

Where can we find creative approaches used by other teams in addressing this issue?

Where can we find a case study of a similar situation?

Who has faced this problem before?

> Prompts: What did they do? What were the results? Has anything been written about best practices or benchmarks in relation to addressing this problem in other organizations?

More questions on learning from others:

_____

_____

_____

_____

_____

_____

Testing Options for Action

To help determine which among various options are most likely to succeed, consider the reasons behind them, the potential impact of decisions, and how options fit with your team strategy or strategic plan (Figure 7.5).

Note: There are a range of questions in this section to support the many possible challenges that facilitators may face when addressing issues. In some situations, a group simply sets criteria for determining a best option and then uses those criteria to select a solution. In other situations, more specific questions are required.

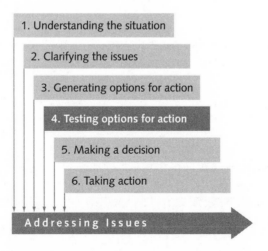

1. Understanding the situation
2. Clarifying the issues
3. Generating options for action
4. Testing options for action
5. Making a decision
6. Taking action

Addressing Issues

Figure 7.5. Testing Options for Action.

Focus: Rationale

Can you help us understand the reasons behind your point of view?

Can you remember our initial reasons for proposing this solution?

How comfortable are you with this option, and why?

How will we know that we have successfully addressed this issue?

> Prompt: What will be different from today?

I'm curious about your reasons for favoring this approach.

What criteria should we consider to narrow down our options?

What do you like most about this solution? What do you like least?

Which of these approaches do you feel most comfortable endorsing? Why?

Which option do you prefer? What are your reasons for supporting this option?

More questions on rationale:

_____

_____

_____

_____

_____

_____

Focus: Potential Impact

How much disruption will this option cause?

> Prompt: How will this disruption likely happen?

If we apply theory X here, what will happen?

If we stay on our current course, what are the implications for our strategic objectives?

If we get a response that says . . . then what will happen to our project?

7

If you take this step, where are you most vulnerable?

If we make this change now, what are some potential immediate, midrange, and long-term impacts for our customers? (*Variation:* Substitute other words for *customers:* "shareholders," "employees," "contributors," "donors.")

What are the benefits and drawbacks of each of these options in relation to your organization?

Where is this solution most vulnerable? That is, if something could go wrong, what would it be?

More questions on potential impact:

_____

_____

_____

_____

_____

_____

Focus: Strategic Fit

How does this option fit with your organizational mission?

>   Prompt: How does it fit with your organizational values?

Which larger systems must be taken into account to support a successful resolution?

Which option fits best with our current infrastructure?

>   Prompt: What infrastructure changes need to be made to support the . . . option?

Which option offers the best chance for success in terms of our strategic direction?

Which options afford a solution for the short run? For the long run?

7

195

Which organization in this partnership has the better resource capacity to follow through on this issue? (*Variation:* Substitute "intellectual," "volunteer," "leadership," "management," "expertise," "human resource," or similar words for *resource.*)

Who might want to protest this option at a political level?

> Prompt: How might we take this knowledge into consideration?

More questions on strategic fit:

_____

_____

_____

_____

_____

_____

Building a lasting consensus is a critical phase in this meeting. Once you have completed the last step in this process, ask group members the following questions:

- Can you live with this action?

- Will you support this action within the group?

- Will you support this action outside the group?

If anyone is unable to answer "yes" to any of the above questions, then ask that person to answer the following questions:

- What has to change in order for you to support this action?

- What might your support look like?

Continue with the decision-making discussion until a proposal is made that meets the conditions for desired changes.

—*Weaver and Farrell, 1997 (adapted)*

7

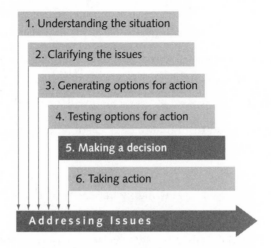

Figure 7.6. Making a Decision.

Making a Decision

According to the criteria you agreed on, which of these three options for action fits best with your strategic direction? (See Figure 7.6.)

Do you get the sense that we are on the same wavelength here, or are we missing each other?

Here is a pattern of questions that facilitators can use with a group to help them make a decision:

1. What are you going to decide?
2. Who will make the decision?
3. What criteria will you use to make your decision?
4. Who is affected by your decision?
5. When must you make your decision?
6. What tool will you use to make your decision?
7. What is your decision at this time? *(Weaver and Farrell, 1997)*

How (for example, group consensus, group vote, senior management authority) should you make this decision?

Is anyone missing from this discussion who might have another perspective? What would this person tell us if she were here?

What action(s) can we take as next steps that will resolve the conflict?

What could prevent you from making a decision about this issue? What factors are supporting you to make a decision now?

What is the decision that you need to make? (*Variation:* "Complete this sentence: We need to decide who . . . will do what . . . by when. . . . " (Weaver and Farrell, 1997)

What is the potential downside of this decision? How can you accommodate it?

What criteria (our values, norms for working together, impact on employees, impact on the public, impact on our stakeholders) can guide us in making our decision?

What are the ethical implications of this decision?

What exactly do we need to decide here?

What is the best way (for example: consensus, voting, multirating) to make this decision?

SCAMPER is a problem-solving technique for use at decision points. The following questions are considered:

S What can be Substituted?

C What can I Combine?

A What can I Adapt?

M How can I Modify or Magnify?

P What can be Put to other uses?

E What can be Eliminated?

R What is a Reverse of the item, or what Rearrangement can be made?

—*Michalko, 1991*

7

What stands out about this option that makes it the best solution?

When does this decision need to be made? Is timing important to the outcome? If yes, how? If no, why not?

Where do we agree? Where do we disagree?

Who is likely to be happy with this solution? Who is likely to be unhappy?

Who will be affected most (or least) by this decision?

> Prompts: How will they be affected? Should we take this information into consideration to make our decision? If so, how?

Whom should you consult with to finalize your decision?

> **Tip: Be clear about your rationale for consultation.**

Who will make the final decision?

> **Tip: Be clear about where the authority for the final decision lies.**

More questions on making a decision:

_____

_____

_____

_____

_____

Taking Action

Taking action on issues requires the engagement of those who will initiate it as well as those who will be affected by it (Figure 7.7). An inclusive approach supports implementation over the long run.

7

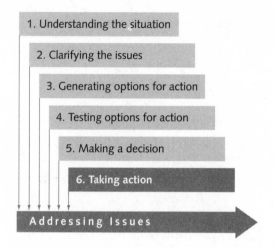

Figure 7.7. Taking Action.

Joseph A. Atkinson, founder of the Toronto Star *daily newspaper, wrote in 1940 that there are four things an executive should know:*

1. What ought to be done?

2. How should it be done?

3. Who should do it?

4. Has it been done?

How can we achieve control in our change strategies without being overly controlling?

How can we be sure that resources allocated to this solution will be distributed fairly?

How can we get our stakeholders involved in the implementation process?

How will this solution affect you personally at work? Focus on specific consequences.

Prompt: How will this solution affect you at home? Focus on specific consequences.

If people are going to resist this solution, what form will that resistance likely take?

Prompt: What is the likely cause of this resistance, and how can we address it?

Is a pilot project needed to test this approach?

On the one hand, the capacity to think and work independently is essential to this change process. The freshest ideas often come from diversity and those marginal to a group. On the other hand, complex change requires many people working insightfully on a solution and acting together. Does our change process honor both individualism and collectivism simultaneously?

What are the top two or three changes that will really challenge productivity while you are moving your headquarters? What do you have going for you that will help you adapt to these changes? What weaknesses does your organization have now that will cause problems in relation to these changes?

What are all the possible ways that this decision could be supported internally?

Prompts: What are all the possible ways that this decision could be thwarted internally? What can we do to address these implementation challenges?

What are our knowledge challenges in following through on this?

Prompts: What do we know that we need to pay special attention to? What don't we know that we need to know? What do others know that we don't know? What are some areas where we may not know what we don't know?

What can we do to facilitate positive politics inside our organization in support of this solution?

What does the research on organizational change recommend regarding the most efficient way to act on our decision?

What factors do we need to consider that could have an impact on a successful implementation?

Prompt: Consider competing priorities, organizational politics, leadership expectations, urgency, resources.

7

201

What is the first thing we need to do to get this solution off on the right foot?

What is our group's role in next steps?

>Prompts: What is our responsibility? What is our accountability?

Where are the traps along the path ahead of us?

>Prompt: What are the supports we can count on along the path ahead of us?

Whom should we involve to support us in being successful?

Who should champion each of the major aspects of this implementation process?

More questions on taking action:

_____

_____

_____

_____

_____

_____

COMMON CHALLENGES

The real-life examples given here explore opportunities for the conscious use of questions in addressing issues.

Encouraging Candor and Confidentiality

Challenge: I often facilitate in situations where I want to encourage candor and confidentiality about issues while maintaining discretion with proprietary or sensitive information. What kinds of questions can I ask to enable this type of environment?

Response: Many facilitated sessions depend on participants disclosing information about their own situation without breaching confidentiality. This can present them with a dilemma: they want to participate in meaningful discussion but at the same time they don't want to betray confidential information about their organization to competitors (see the discussion in Chapter Two about clarifying confidentiality). They may also not want to portray their organization in a negative light.

Although setting a norm for candor can be a good start, as a facilitator you may find that it doesn't work unless the questions used during the session reinforce that norm by stimulating appropriate disclosure from participants.

A climate that supports appropriate disclosure is one in which ground rules for confidentiality are in place, information sharing is a norm, the facilitator models appropriate information sharing (that is, not disclosing names of other clients, upholding mutual respect), questions are constructed to "protect" the participant while she is disclosing information, and mistakes are seen as an opportunity for learning.

Here are sample questions that support participants in disclosing appropriately:

What's one thing you know for sure about this issue?

What's one thing you learned as a result of your experience as a senior manager in large organizations?

From your perspective, what is at stake here for employees?

If you could predict the top two (human resource) issues for organizations like yours over the next five years, what would they be?

Most managers today are experiencing the fallout of this issue. Is this a challenge in your organization? What symptoms do you notice?

What's one perspective you are hearing about these days in relation to these issues?

Putting Sensitive Issues on the Table

Challenge: What questions can I ask to get participants' views about a sensitive issue (such as gender equity) on the table during a mixed (male and female) group discussion?

7

Response: Split participants into two groups, the men and the women. Ask each group to complete a given sentence by making a list on a flipchart (Tomlinson and Strachan, 1991). The women's group completes the sentence, "In our society, being a woman can mean that. . . ." The men's group completes the sentence, "In our society, being a man can mean that. . . ." (Customize the sentence to suit your situation.) Then each group presents its list and the facilitator asks participants to comment on impressions, surprises, omissions, additions, and so on while discussing similarities and differences between the two lists.

The purpose of this activity is to explore differences, not to create an argument about what is right or wrong or which way is best. If there are differing points of view, acknowledge them and continue with the discussion rather than trying to resolve them.

Issues Management in a Nongovernmental Organization

Many organizations also have their own established approaches to addressing issues. In the nongovernmental sector, agencies are often well organized with respect to issues management, as is illustrated by the approach in the Kidney Foundation of Canada's Advocacy Handbook.

Successful advocacy requires a proactive and systematic approach to issues management, usually over an extended period of time. The first four steps should be part of the ongoing activities of an advocacy group. The last three steps will be most important when the need to take action has been identified and agreed upon.

1. Gathering intelligence: What's going on out there?
2. Building relationships: Who should we be talking to?
3. Identifying and analyzing the issues: Whose problem is it anyway?
4. Researching the issues: What else do we need to know?
5. Developing a position: What are we going to say?
6. Developing and implementing a strategy: What are we going to do?
7. Evaluating the outcome: Are we there yet?

—*Kidney Foundation of Canada, Advocacy Handbook, 1999*

7

204

Issues-Based Planning: A Redundancy Program

Challenge: A strategic review conducted by the management of a large UK company led to systematic reduction in the number of employees across the company. The staff association—comprising more than eighty representatives—felt powerless to help its members through implementation of a management-led redundancy program. As an internal consultant/facilitator, the challenge for me was to help staff members understand what had happened and learn from what was at times an unpleasant experience.

Response: The sponsor wanted all representatives to have an opportunity to be involved in addressing this challenge. He was also concerned that negative experiences would dominate the process and that people would find it difficult to let go and move on.

After some discussion, we decided to (1) survey everybody and (2) using the survey results hold a review workshop—all representatives were invited to attend—to discuss common concerns and suggest ways to move forward.

We wanted the survey to go beyond the standard questions ("What worked well?" "What didn't work?" "What could we do differently?") to more specific and engaging questions. To do this, we used the What?—So what?—Now what? process framework of Chapter Five and the "addressing issues" framework of this chapter as a guide for developing the survey:

1. What are the first words that come to mind to describe how you felt as a representative when this program was announced?

2. What are the first words that come to mind to describe how you feel now?

3. On a scale of 1 to 10 (where 10 is totally effective), how effective were we during the consultation process?

4. Describe how effective we were in challenging decisions made by the company.

5. On a scale of 1 to 10 (where 10 is totally prepared), how prepared were you to undertake this role?

6. Describe how the spirit of the partnership agreement was evident in your dealings with local management throughout the consultation period.

7. What support did you need to carry out your role?

7

8. What support did you provide to staff?

9. On a scale of 1 to 10 (where 10 is excellent), how effective were we in providing this support?

10. What was reasonable about the restrictions on communication?

11. What was unreasonable about the restrictions on communication?

12 On a scale of 1 to 10 (where 10 is excellent), how well did we communicate with each other during this program?

13. On a scale of 1 to 10 (where 10 is excellent), how well did we communicate with staff during this program?

14 How could we have improved the way we communicated?

15. What are some positive things that happened to you as a result of your participation in this program?

16 What are some negative things that happened to you as a result of your participation in this program?

17. When you look back at your experience during the program, what did you learn about the role of a representative?

18. If you were developing a training program for representatives, what would you recommend based on your experience of this program?

19. If you had to do this all again next week, what is the one thing you would change?

20. On a scale of 1 to 10 (where 10 is totally confident), how confident do you think the staff were in our ability to help and support them throughout this program?

21. On a scale of 1 to 10 (where 10 is excellent), overall how well did we carry out our role during this program?

7

All the representatives responded to every question within a two-week timeframe. Some wrote lengthy responses ("War and Peace") and many others were not shy about using expletives to explain how they felt in response to question 1.

I consolidated the responses into an anonymous thirty-five-page report, carefully retaining duplications and expletives. This summary was distributed to everyone one week prior to a one-day review workshop attended by approximately fifty representatives.

We spent the morning in small teams identifying key themes, using the survey results as a guide. In the afternoon, we worked on a plan for changing how the association would operate in the future. This plan included fundamental changes in the relationship between the association and the management team, how the association developed and supported its representatives, and how communication channels could be improved.

The workshop was well received. Feedback included these comments:

- "I didn't believe we could get so much out on the table."

- "The questions were really challenging and thought provoking."

- "For the first time we have all been given the opportunity to contribute to the future of the association and we feel we have all been listened to."

- "We really identified the key challenges and the actions we need to take."

(This challenge was provided by the internal facilitator and change consultant of the company.)

7

8 Questions for Closing a Session

Although often neglected, a closing is as important as an opening.

At the end of a single session or a longer process involving multiple meetings, the challenge for the facilitator is to bring closure to the process. Participants need to reflect on what they have accomplished and on what they want to do next in relation to their objectives.

Closing questions also help participants reenter their day-to-day work patterns in the context of the meeting or workshop they are completing. Thus closing questions are often a bridge between the end of one process and the beginning of another (for example, the end of strategic planning and the beginning of operational planning).

PROCESS FRAMEWORK

The process framework in Figure 8.1 is a guide for developing questions to close a process, whether it consists of a single workshop or a series of sessions. The emphasis in this framework is twofold: looking backward (wrapping up the process) and looking forward (considering next steps). The Janus icon in Figure 8.1 represents the Ancient Roman god of gates and doorways, beginnings and endings.

1. Looking Backward	2. Looking Forward
• Midway through a process • The experience as a whole • Learning • Productivity • Management of the process	• Celebrating success • Building ownership for follow-through • Taking action—knowledge translation • Future collaboration

Figure 8.1. Process Framework for Closing a Session.

Although (as mentioned in the Preface) the questions in this chapter are designed for verbal interaction during a session, they can also be adapted for written feedback forms.

GUIDELINES FOR QUESTIONS TO CLOSE A SESSION

Closing questions are transitional; they are the key to addressing unfinished business and moving on. They also create a special opportunity for learning as participants close their "files" on a process and decide what to do next.

• Create closing questions that support participants in bringing an end to a process. These questions assist participants in summarizing what they have or have not achieved with respect to their stated objectives ("What did we do best during this process?" "What could we have done better?").

• Ask questions that support discussion about various perspectives on the conclusion of a process. Some participants may want to postpone the ending of a workshop; others may be glad to see it ending. If you are bringing closure to a lengthy and involved process after which people will no longer be seeing each other, some participants may want to discuss their feelings about leaving each other or communicating less frequently, or they may want to set up a network.

• Ensure that responses to closing questions feed into the client-consultant debriefing meeting for a project ("If you were the facilitator for this session, what is one thing you would do differently next time?").

8

• Ask questions that encourage recognition of the contributions of everyone involved in the project or meeting ("What did you learn from each other as colleagues during this project?").

• Enable participants to feel included as legitimate members of the group who brought something meaningful to the discussion ("What is one contribution or perspective that you brought to the table?").

• Consider whether it is appropriate to create an opportunity for participants to respond to questions confidentially, as through an anonymous written questionnaire.

• Use questions that encourage participants to disclose their concerns, anxieties, and areas of disagreement in a nonthreatening, low-anxiety manner ("You can help us learn by describing how this process went for you. What did you like most about this session? What did you like least?").

• Develop questions that move participants through the What?—So what?—Now what? framework of Chapter Five and that promote a positive and motivating link into next steps or future sessions.

• Ensure that the time allotted for the closing is appropriate given the relationship between what people want to say and how their comments tie into the session objectives and overall purpose. In some situations, the answers to closing questions need to be extremely short, perhaps five to ten seconds per person ("Let's go around the table and say what single word or phrase describes your experience here today. Give us the first one that comes to mind right now; don't think about it. It's OK if your word is the same as someone else's.")

QUESTION BANK

More than one wise person has commented on the fact that an unexamined life is not worth living. So it goes with processes and facilitation.

The questions in this bank can be customized for a range of situations: closing a workshop, engaging planning committee members in a debriefing meeting, concluding a series of meetings, wrapping up a large conference, facilitating a debriefing session with clients, and so on. Be sure to customize the questions to suit your specific situation.

8

Looking Backward

The questions given here encourage participants (either individually or as a group) to think about the process at a midway point and at the end (Figure 8.2).

Focus: Midway Through a Process

If you could change one thing about today's session, what would it be? (*Variation:* Substitute other words or phrases for *today's*, such as "this morning's" or "our past.")

On a scale of 1 to 4, where 1 is poor and 4 is excellent, how would you describe today?" (*Variation:* Substitute other words or phrases for *today*, such as "this morning" or "this last session.")

> Prompt: What could you (or we) do to change this number for tomorrow?

Were there specific times during the first part of this event when you were aware of having heightened emotions?

> Prompt: What is your perspective on those times now that we are halfway through?

What are you going to focus on during tomorrow's session?

1. Looking Backward	2. Looking Forward
• Midway through a process • The experience as a whole • Learning • Productivity • Management of the process	• Celebrating success • Building ownership for follow-through • Taking action—knowledge translation • Future collaboration

Figure 8.2. Looking Backward.

8

What are you going to focus on in relation to . . . as a result of participating in this session?

What is one thing that stood out for you during today's session?

What is one thing you can learn from someone else in your group during the time remaining in this process?

What possible issues, if any, do you see emerging?

What was the most relevant part of this experience for you?

What were your recurring thoughts during today's small-group session?

> Prompt: Did your thoughts help or hinder your participation?

More questions for midway through a process:

_____

_____

_____

_____

_____

_____

Focus: The Experience as a Whole

After participating on this team for an entire season, what do you think are the coach's key values or deeply held beliefs about working with high-performance athletes? (*Variation:* Substitute "manager" or "leader" for *coach* and adjust the end of the question to suit your situation.)

Do you feel any different about yourself as a team member after working on this project for six months?

From your perspective, how does a really excellent process differ from one that is second-rate?

How clear was the purpose of this session during the first few hours?

How comfortable are you with how tensions and disagreements were handled by group members? Please explain.

8

How comfortable are you with the level of participation by group members?

How creative were we in our approach to issues? (*Variations:* Substitute other words for *creative:* "timely," "focused," "candid," "pragmatic.")

How did other participants contribute to your experience during this course?

> Prompt: What did they contribute that helped or hindered you in having a successful and enjoyable course?

How was disagreement or tension handled in your small group?

> Prompts: What was your level of comfort with tension among group members? Was it dealt with constructively? Were there situations where it became destructive?

How well did we listen to each other throughout this process?

If a couple of your best friends were going to come into this account planning session next year, what advice would you give them about how to have a successful and enjoyable planning session?

In hindsight, what two or three core values guided how your group functioned?

Looking back on this process, what's the good news?

> Prompts: What's the bad news? Did people participate equally? Did some people avoid participating?

On a scale of 1 to 5, where 1 is poor and 5 is excellent, how would you describe today?

> Prompts: What made you pick that number? Is this the number you usually pick to describe your days, or do the numbers vary? Do you want to change this number for tomorrow? What could you (or we) do to change this number for tomorrow?

Overall, how did this process go for you?

> Prompt: What were the strong and weak parts of it, from your perspective?

What are the first words that come to mind to describe how you felt when this session started?

> Prompt: What are the first words that come to mind to describe how you feel now?

> **Tip: If you used the first question during the opening part of the session, refer to those responses at the end for additional comments.**

What benefits did you experience as a result of being involved with this project?

What could have made this experience more meaningful for you?

What did this session feel like to you?

What did you like most about this meeting? What did you like least?

> **Tip: This question also works well for long-term project closings. For example, "What did you like most [or least] about being involved in this project over the past six months?"**

What do you know now that you didn't know when this process started?

What influences outside your work environment had a positive effect on your experience as a team member for this project?

> Prompt: What influences outside your work environment had a negative effect on your experiences as a team member for this project?

What stands out most in your mind about this session?

What themes kept emerging in discussion during the last part of the process?

> Prompt: Why do you think these themes came to the fore?

8

What was the most valuable aspect of this experience for you?

What's one good thing that happened for you today? What's one not-so-good thing?

When (how often) did personalities get in the way of constructive problem solving?

Would you describe the level of tension on your team during this project as low, medium, or high? Please explain your response.

More questions on the experience as a whole:

_____

_____

_____

_____

_____

_____

Focus: Learning

Did we have the right people involved to achieve our stated objectives?

> Prompts: If yes, please describe the roles (skills, characteristics) required that were fulfilled by team members. If no, please suggest additional roles (skills, characteristics) required. From this discussion, what have we learned for next time?

Distribute completed evaluation sheets to the organizational team and ask, "What do our evaluations say about how this project went?"

> Prompts: If you were planning a project similar to this one, what would you do the same? What would you do differently?

From your perspective, what was this group best at?

> Prompts: Where was this group weakest? How are these conclusions instructive for next time?

Has your perception of this issue changed throughout this process?

> Prompts: If yes, how? If no, why do you think it didn't change?

Hindsight takes reflection to become 20/20. If you were facilitating this process next year, what would you change?

> Prompt: What would you keep the same?

If a colleague asked you what you learned from being involved in this session, what would you say?

If you were the senior manager looking back on this project, what is one thing you would do differently that could have a significant positive impact on the outcome?

How did you find this process similar to your work situation?

> Prompt: How was it different?

Looking back, which results (if any) were predictable?

> Prompt: Did any surprise you?

What have we learned that we can take forward into the next session on this project?

> Prompts: What would we do differently? What would we keep the same? What helped us? What hindered us?

What is one thing you have learned from working with the people on this team?

> Prompt: What do you think you have learned as a team within your larger organization?

What went wrong? What went right? What went so-so?

> Prompt for each question: How did that happen?

8

When did you feel most engaged in this event? least engaged? (*Variation:* Substitute other words for *engaged*, such as "comfortable" or "uncomfortable," "productive" or "unproductive.")

> Prompt: Why do you think this was so?

More questions on learning:

_____

_____

_____

_____

_____

_____

Focus: Productivity

During introductions you were asked about your hopes and concerns for this meeting. How did the meeting turn out for you in terms of what you hoped for?

Have you achieved the objectives or outcomes stated at the beginning of this process?

> Prompt: If yes, how do you know? If no, what else needs to be done to achieve these objectives or outcomes?

Have we addressed all the main issues?

How did the small group session work for you: were you in a stimulating and productive group or not?

> Prompt: Tell me more.

How did your group make key decisions? Did this work well?

8

How does our final product (result) compare with our initial ideas and objectives?

> Prompts: Have we kept on track? Is the difference primarily an improvement or a problem?

How would you describe the contribution we have made to this area as a result of this process?

> Prompt: Would you describe our contribution differently to various individuals or groups? Why or why not?

Now that the main workshop is over, what unfinished business do you think this group still needs to address?

Now that we have completed our discussion on . . . how confident are you with the decisions we have made?

On a scale of 1 to 4, where 1 is not successful and 4 is successful, how would you describe what we accomplished with respect to each of our objectives?

On a scale of 1 to 4, where 1 is not successful and 4 is successful, how successful was this session in terms of productivity, from your perspective? Please explain. (*Variations:* Substitute other words or phrases for *how successful was this session:* "how well did this session meet our objectives," "how healthy were your interactions as group members.")

To what extent did you achieve your personal objectives for this session?

What are you most concerned about now that this process is over?

What did you contribute to the session's outcomes (to the group's productivity)?

> *Focus on guidelines for effective feedback to ensure that the debriefing doesn't become superficial or negative.*

What do we still need to talk about to be able to move this forward?

What happened in this process that you thought would happen?

> Prompt: What happened that surprised you?

8

What is one immediate output from this process that is of value from your perspective?

> Prompts: What is one long-term outcome from this process that is of value from your perspective? What indicators could you use to measure this value over three months, six months, one year?

What is one thing you learned about information technology planning through your involvement in this project? (*Variations:* Substitute other words or phrases for *information technology planning,* such as "social support networks," "leadership development," "strategic planning," "project management.")

What opportunities did we act on that helped us do this work?

> Prompt: Did we miss any opportunities that could have improved the outcome?

What turning points did you notice during this process?

> Prompt: Do we have any undiscussables that still require work?

What were your goals at the beginning of the day?

> Prompt: To what extent did you achieve them?

Which of your norms for working together helped your group the most in terms of productivity?

> Prompt: How did they help?

You have been approached by an auditor who is investigating the usefulness of this process in relation to the amount of money invested in making it happen. What would you say to the auditor?

8

More questions on productivity:

_____

_____

_____

_____

_____

_____

Focus: Management of the Process

Did you have the support (human and financial resources, technology, political) required for this process to be successful? Please explain.

Do you have any regrets about how this process was managed—location, scheduling, accommodation, food, furniture? (*Variation:* Substitute other words for *management,* such as "facilitated" or "initiated.")

How did the room setup contribute to or detract from a successful workshop? (Strachan and Pitters, 2003)

Was there anything in our approach that you found frustrating?

What was your favorite part of how this process was managed?

> Prompt: What did you like least?

More questions on management of the process:

_____

_____

_____

_____

_____

_____

8

Looking Forward

People who attend a lot of meetings, planning workshops, and training sessions may become quite cynical about the value of the process if there is no follow-up action based on what was accomplished. The questions suggested by Figure 8.3 help to bridge the potential gap between the facilitated process and the follow-up action.

Focus: Celebrating Success

How can we celebrate what we have accomplished? How can we celebrate how we worked together?

How can we formally declare that this project is now completed? (*Variation:* "How can we celebrate the conclusion of this project?")

What is one takeaway or significant benefit you got out of today's session? (*Variation:* "What is one thing of value that you are walking away with as a result of participating in this process?")

What parts of your involvement in this program did you find the most fun?

> Prompt: What happened that made them fun? (*Variation:* Substitute other words for *fun,* such as "productive," "enjoyable," "educational," "stimulating," "troubling.")

What positive ripple effects might our initiative have?

Whom do we want to acknowledge for their effort and accomplishments in making this event successful?

More questions on celebrating success:

_____

_____

_____

_____

_____

_____

8

1. Looking Backward	2. Looking Forward
• Midway through a process • The experience as a whole • Learning • Productivity • Management of the process	• Celebrating success • Building ownership for follow-through • Taking action—knowledge translation • Future collaboration

Figure 8.3. Looking Forward.

Focus: Building Ownership for Follow-Through

For additional questions, see Chapters Five and Seven.

How interested are you in continuing your involvement with the next steps in this process?

If you were going to offer this session again in three months, what would you include in your recipe for success?

Should we be accountable to one another in any way after this workshop is over? If yes, why? If no, why not?

> Prompt: If you are uncomfortable with some aspect of the process just completed, how could we address that before moving forward?

What aspects of this plan will take courage to implement?

> Prompts: Why? How can we address this?

What is one thing you will do as a result of this session once you are back in your office?

What legacy would your team like to leave behind for your organization?

What will you stop, start, or continue doing as a result of your involvement in this event?

Where and how could we let ourselves down in relation to next steps?

8

Prompt: What do we need to do to prevent this from happening?

Who needs to work with us on *what* to achieve *which outcome?*

Prompt: How can we engage them in this?

Would you like to be involved in the implementation part of this process?

Prompts: If yes, please explain how you might contribute. If no, please explain why not.

You have just spent two days discussing how our company acts on its corporate social responsibility in this community. If you were in charge of this organization, what is the first thing you would do to act on the results of this session?

Prompt: How can we support this coming about if we are not in charge?

More questions on building ownership for follow-through:

_____

_____

_____

_____

_____

_____

Focus: Taking Action—Knowledge Translation

Taking action happens in many forms, such as communication initiatives, policy development and implementation, creation of new standards, changes in group norms, revisions to existing protocols, and where there is a focus on learning.

Knowledge translation (also called knowledge transfer) is a form of action that focuses on closing the gap between *what we know* on the basis of research and experience in an area and *what we do* in daily situations to apply that knowledge. Professional associations and societies are particularly focused on knowledge translation in relation to decisions affecting the quality of their services.

8

Many of the questions in this section address more than one way to take action; for example, knowledge translation may also involve policy development and a related communication initiative.

After all is said and done, what did we learn through the research part of this initiative that we need to act on as soon as possible?

Are there other areas of our organization or related organizations that would appreciate learning from our experience?

> Prompt: What have we learned that could be applicable to them?

Given the nature of our conclusions and the risks involved in implementation, what is the best pace for moving forward?

How can we secure resources to support next steps?

How can we share what we have learned from this project with others inside and outside our organization who could benefit from our experience?

> Prompt: Who might be interested?

How is our experience relevant to those with whom we collaborate? (*Variation:* "Are we in any partnership or alliance that would appreciate hearing about our experience?

> Prompt: What would they like to know?

How much healthy tension do you think is attached to implementation of our work?

> Prompts: How much unhealthy tension do we need to consider? How can we take this into consideration during next steps?

If you were in charge, what is one thing you would do to build on the work that has already been done?

Is there a journal, magazine, or internal newsletter that would be interested in publishing a short article describing our experience and what we have learned from this process?

8

Now that this project is completed, as project team members we will be taking the results of our work back to our various departments in the company. How do we want to talk about what happened during this start-up phase?

> Prompt: What can we do as a group to support a common leadership message about resource planning?

> **Tip: Project teams can play a large role in an organization in relation to implementation. Common messages help support the next steps.**

So, what do we need to do next here?

There is often a large gap between what we know as a result of a session like this and what we practice. Who else could we involve that might help us translate our decisions into real change in the field?

What are the requirements for turning our recommendations into standards of practice?

What do we need to do to ensure that our recommendations are brought before the legislature for political support?

What happens after a retreat is often as important as what happens during it. In your view, what next steps need to take place to ensure successful follow-through?

What single factor is most important in determining whether our organization is successful in acting on the recommendations?

What mechanisms are needed to sustain this initiative in our rapidly changing environment?

What will you persuade your organization to stop, start, or continue doing . . . as a result of your involvement in this event?

Which professional societies or associations might be interested in what we have done and how it applies to our profession?

Who are our publics? How should we communicate with them about this process?

Who has the positional power to implement our conclusions?

More questions on taking action and knowledge translation:

_____

_____

_____

_____

_____

Focus: Future Collaboration

Given the discussion between our two organizations today, what does Organization A bring to the table that is unique to it and would be beneficial to Organization B? What does B bring to the table that is unique to it and would be beneficial to A?

> Prompt: How can we bring these organizations together for mutual benefit?

Given the results of this process, have we made any promises to supporters or stakeholders that we need to act on or reconsider as we go forward?

What implications do our decisions have for what needs to happen next in our community?

What other organizations are you aware of that might benefit from your experience in, and the conclusion to, this process?

> Prompt: Would they like to meet with us to share experiences, lessons learned, and areas for mutual growth and development?

Which communities, groups, teams, and departments should we connect with for support in implementing our decisions?

8

More questions on future collaboration:

_____

_____

_____

_____

_____

COMMON CHALLENGES

The next examples explore opportunities for conscious use of closing questions to address typical challenges encountered by facilitators.

Bringing a Multisite Project to a Close

Challenge: I am an external management consultant who has just completed implementation of a new information technology (IT) reengineering process in a national firm with nine locations in our country. This process, sponsored by the firm's human resources area, began with all nine teams together at a two-day national meeting. Then we worked with each team onsite to support them in providing local leadership over a period of three months.

We are bringing the nine teams together again in two weeks for a meeting to discuss how the project has unfolded and to bring closure to this training process. Four internal human resource (HR) people will also be present at this meeting. The IT project will be formally handed over to these teams for implementation. Each team has five to seven members, depending on the size of their location.

What questions might be helpful at this closing session?

Response: The first step is to consult with the sponsor (HR) to discuss their expectations and clarify possible outcomes. There are several possible purposes for this event:

- To bring everyone together in a joint learning session

- To bring formal closure to the project

228

- To develop a report on lessons learned so that the CEO can share this information with other CEOs at the quarterly international executives' meeting

- To end the project on a positive note

- To explore unfinished business among team members and between teams

- To provide a venue where the president can make a formal presentation to reward successful team work

- To thank team members for their efforts

- To think about next steps in maintaining and enhancing the new IT approach on an ongoing basis

If the purpose of the meeting is to acknowledge and celebrate what the teams have accomplished, you may want them to sit in their work teams to address questions at the beginning of the meeting and then move them out of those teams during further discussions. In this way, they have an initial opportunity to be acknowledged as a working group and celebrate their accomplishments while then moving on to reidentify with the larger group toward the end of the session.

The questions in teams could ask them to reflect on their experience in working together—for example, what the key challenges were and what they can celebrate now that their work is completed. The questions in the larger group could provide feedback to HR for future projects of this scope ("Given hindsight, if you were in charge, what is one thing you would do to enhance the ability of team members to work together efficiently and successfully?").

Here are further sample questions for this closing session, depending on your purpose. Some of these questions may also be appropriate for a written questionnaire sent to participants before the actual session.

Here are the objectives for this closing session. Do they seem appropriate to you? Please comment, making additions or deletions if you wish.

If you had to do this all over again next week, what is one thing you would change?

What did you like most about being a member of your location's team?

What do we still have to work on?

8

What went well on this project?

You have been promoted to director of HR for the western regions of your company. Your first major task is to develop and implement a process similar to this one. What have you learned from this process that will help you in your new position? State each learning in a single sentence, as a commandment, beginning with a verb.

Closing a National, Issues-Based Workshop

Challenge: I am facilitating a national workshop on transportation issues for an arms-length Crown corporation. There are forty-five participants from all sectors of the economy: private, public, union, and nongovernmental groups. What suggestions do you have for closing questions?

Response: In situations similar to this one, we have set two or three closing questions and then tested them with a representative volunteer from each sector during the final workshop break to ensure that the questions are appropriate. A representative planning committee might also be a good place to test the questions prior to using them.

Taking a consultative approach to developing these questions helps to ensure that you avoid bias or any accusation that the questions were set to make the workshop outcomes look good.

Option A: Ask people to sit in their four sector teams and come to agreement in ten minutes on responses to these questions:

What is one thing that stood out for you at this meeting in relation to how people worked together?

What message will you be taking back to your sector's organization?

Then ask a volunteer from each sector team to present the results to the total group. You can close with the committee chair thanking the participants, presenters, and others and reviewing the agreed next steps.

Option B: The closure to a workshop is often the ending of one phase and the starting up of another. Workshops usually generate work for specific people, and there is a need to communicate with those who weren't there. An important question to ask is, "How can we communicate with others who aren't here to ensure that they hear about the workshop and its impact in their part of the country?" One solution is a phone or e-mail tree: each person contacts one or two other people to tell them about the results of the workshop. As part of your debriefing activity, you can develop the key points that would be part of what people tell one another.

Option C: At a national network meeting where the purpose was to extend the network from a fairly closed partnership of four large agencies to a broader partnership involving seventeen various agencies (also in the workshop), we asked one representative from each agency in the room to deliver the closing remarks by talking about one thing they learned at the event and how they thought their organization might want to participate in the network in the future.

This closing (Option C) promoted the goals of the workshop by emphasizing the importance of an inclusive approach. In addition, it avoided having the original four larger partners, who gave the opening remarks, also give the closing remarks. The approach worked well; several people commented on how powerful they found the closing comments of the seventeen participating agencies.

Conducting Exit Interviews in Small Groups

(Note: This challenge is adapted from Tomlinson and Strachan, 1996, pp. 64–65.)

Challenge: I am the coach of a national women's sports team. This year we are dropping six athletes from our roster. One has been the team captain for three years, two have been on the team for four years, and two others are subs who have had very little match playing time. I am going to conduct final interviews with the athletes in small groups and am having difficulty thinking of suitable questions. How should I set this up?

Response: Athletes and coaches learn a lot through their participation in sports. You and they both can benefit from sharing those learnings and passing them on to future coaches and athletes. Interviews that wrap up an athlete's career are important for several reasons:

8

- Athletes will be better able to integrate the value of their athletic experience into their lives after sports if they are encouraged to reflect on its potential impact and meaning.

- Final interviews are an opportunity for you to address unfinished business, challenges that you and the athletes may have experienced and not talked through completely.

- Athletes who reflect on and value their experience in sports may be potential coaches; no sport can afford to overlook an opportunity to encourage the future involvement of former athletes.

How you describe these group interviews and set them up and how you plan to use the resulting feedback influences the quality of participation. Be sure to explain that these are confidential small-group discussions (see Chapter Two, discussion about clarifying confidentiality), that you will be reporting back to the entire team (including those interviewed) with an anonymous summary of what was said, and that you will be integrating as many suggestions as possible with next season's team.

> **Tip: Pay attention to the type and order of questions (see Chapter One, "Skills for Conscious Questioning" section). After the interviews are completed, give players a couple of examples of changes you will be making.**

Here are some suggested questions:

Do you have any regrets about your participation as a member of this team?

> Prompts: What did you do that you might have done differently? Do you have any heightened feelings about others on the team? Do you need to have any closing discussions with people on the team about things that happened?

If you could change one key thing you did during your participation in this sport, what would it be?

8

If you could experience one thing again that you experienced while you were participating in this sport, what would that be?

> Prompt: Do you want to share these feelings with others who were involved with you at the time?

If you had a child who wanted to get involved in competitive sports, what would you consider before signing her up?

Suppose you are developing a training program for coaches. What courses come to mind as being most important?

Overall, on a scale of 1 to 6, where 1 is poor and 6 is excellent, how would you describe your experience as a . . . player? Please explain your choice of number.

Sports create many pressures for athletes. Describe one positive pressure and a negative one that you experienced.

Think of all the athletes you have known during your experience in sports. Pick one that you especially admire. In your view, what is it about this athlete that makes her admirable?

Think of all the coaches you have had. Pick one who was particularly effective. In your view, what was it about this coach that made her effective?

Was it your choice to get involved in our sport, or was someone else behind getting you involved?

What are some memorable things that have happened to you as a result of your participation in this sport?

What are some positive things that have happened to you as a result of your participation in this sport?

What did you learn about coaching as a result of participating in this sport?

What did you learn about yourself as a result of participating in this sport?

What did you learn as a result of your experiences in this sport that you can apply in other situations?

What did you want when you first signed up?

> Prompt: Did you get it?

8

233

What were some highlights for you as an athlete in this sport?

What were you looking for when you first got involved in this sport?

> Prompt: Has what you were looking for changed or evolved while you were playing?

Reviewing a Pilot Workshop

Challenge: I am looking for some questions to ask participants at the end of a one-day pilot workshop on benchmarking. This workshop will be revised on the basis of participants' feedback and then offered at multiple sites to middle managers, all of whom are required to participate in a workshop within a four-month period.

Response: When introducing questions, remind participants that this is a pilot workshop that will be reviewed, refined, and then offered at other sites. Ask them to contribute their expertise to the review process by responding to your questions. Use the list given here to create three or four questions that focus directly on your review process.

As you know, we are going to be providing this workshop to all middle managers over the next four months. We want to build ownership and commitment to using benchmarking regularly. What advice do you have for us as organizers now that you have completed this session?

Given your experience, what do you think are the key points that facilitators should be emphasizing in this workshop?

How will you report back to your supervisor on this workshop?

How will you portray this workshop to other managers? Why so? (*Variation:* Replace *other managers* with "supervisors" or "fellow employees.")

We are interested in having people with your experience as trained facilitators for this initiative. Are you interested in taking a two-day training session and then cofacilitating a workshop to be based on a revised agenda?

> Prompt: Can you recommend other managers at your level who might be interested in cofacilitating these workshops?

8

What do you think is the main factor in your company that will determine whether benchmarking is an overall success?

> Prompt: What can we do through these workshops to ensure that this factor is addressed?

What is one question you had about benchmarking that was answered during this workshop?

> Prompt: What is one unanswered question you still have at the end of this workshop?

Will you change anything in terms of how you act back home on the basis of your participation in this workshop?

> Prompt: Ask for specific examples.

8

In Closing:
About Questions—
What I Know for Sure

A question that usually works well for me when facilitating is, "What is one thing you know for sure about . . . ?" It seems fitting that in closing this book I try to answer it. What do I know for sure about making questions work in facilitated sessions?

- *The more you know, the more focused and productive your questions will be.* Although it is true that you can facilitate a session in an area you know little about, you can add significant value by making sure you know the basics: the purpose and objectives of a session, the people involved, the current situation and related facilitation challenges, and the process frameworks required to address the facilitation challenges.

In addition to the basic elements, be familiar with these other aspects of an area: key related organizations and their leaders, current issues and associated considerations, assumptions underlying the process, affiliated systems in various sectors, areas of recent media attention, key technical words and their meanings, commonly used acronyms, recent articles and opinion pieces on the topic, and potential areas for conflict of interest among those involved. Finally, it is essential to know as much as possible

> *Curious people love questions. Looking for questions for a session is a great way to cultivate your curiosity about an area in which you are working.*

about yourself as a facilitator—strengths, weaknesses, perspectives, and values. (See Chapter One for a discussion of conscious questioning.)

• *Facilitators can recognize the right questions.* If you know what you need to know about a specific situation, you can browse through a book like this one and recognize what you need to ask. You

> *The more you understand, the better you can "stand under" the process and enable it to work.*

may not see the exact question right away, but simply by flipping through the section that applies to the process framework you need, you will recognize key elements and related ideas so that you can quickly customize an example or craft your own question to suit your situation.

An effective facilitator recognizes when questions are stale. If you are tired of using the same old questions to open a session or uncover supports and barriers, push yourself to try something new. What may feel risky initially—trying out new questions—often results in increased confidence and creativity as you watch those questions do their work with a group.

• *Your intuition can be trusted.* I spend more time on the questions that drive an agenda than I do on almost any other aspect of designing a process. Even so,

> In all affairs it's a healthy thing now and then to hang a question mark on the things you have long taken for granted.
>
> —Bertrand Russell

sometimes a client signs off on the questions and thinks they're right on target, but I still feel uneasy. There could be any number of reasons for this concern: Is there enough time to do the question justice? Does the question have too much risk for where it is situated in the agenda? Has the question

already been answered in a previous session? Is the question at the right level for these participants?

Regardless of the reason, trust your feelings and review the question again. You might do so by exploring possible answers with your client or planning committee, or by checking out the question with a colleague.

• *The right questions enable learning.* Most facilitators I know like to learn. They also enjoy enabling others to learn. As participants make decisions that work well for them, they learn. When people work together in groups, they learn. The right questions enable individuals, groups, and organizations to have meaningful learning experiences, particularly in relation to the purpose and outcomes of a process.

Workshops and longer processes are conducive to a positive learning experience if the participants have a commitment to what is being discussed and to what will happen as a result of the process; if they are engaged in productive discussion and relationships that enable them to meet the goals for both

> The important thing is not to stop questioning. Curiosity has its own reason for existing. One cannot help but be in awe when he contemplates the mysteries of eternity, of life, of the marvelous structure of reality. It is enough if one tries merely to comprehend a little of this mystery every day. Never lose a holy curiosity.
>
> —*Albert Einstein*

the process and their own development; and if the process environment is comfortable, mutually respectful, and candid. In such a situation, effective questioning pays big learning dividends for individuals, groups and organizations.

Learning about ourselves as facilitators comes from recognizing our own questions. What questions about how you facilitate would you like to explore over the next few years?

_____

_____

_____

_____

_____

_____

Date: _____

> *Facilitation is about learning to love all the questions, both the ones we ask ourselves and those we ask others.*

References

"Albert Einstein quotes." *ThinkExist.com Quotatrions online.* [http://en.thinkexist.com/quotes/albert_einstein/].

Argyris, C. *Intervention Theory and Method: A Behavioral Science View.* Reading, Mass.: Addison-Wesley, 1970.

Argyris, C. *Strategy, Change, and Defensive Routines.* Boston: Pittman, 1985.

Bens, I. *Facilitating with Ease!* San Francisco: Jossey-Bass, 2000.

Bloom, B. S. *Taxonomy of Educational Objectives, Handbook I: The Cognitive Domain.* New York: McKay, 1956.

Bonhoeffer, D. "Suum Cuique." *Ethics,* 1955. (Reprint, London: SCM Press, 1993.) As quoted in J. Dalla Costa, *The Ethical Imperative: Why Moral Leadership Is Good Business.* New York: HarperCollins, 1998.

Bradbury, R. *Fahrenheit 451: The Temperature at Which Books Burn.* New York: Ballantine Books, 1950.

Brockman, J. (ed. and pub.). *The Edge Annual Question-2005.* Edge: World Question Center. [http://www.edge.org/q2005/q05_print.html]. 2005.

Brookfield, S. D. *Developing Critical Thinkers.* San Francisco: Jossey-Bass, 1987.

Christensen, C., Gavin, D. A., and Sweet, A. *Education for Judgement: The Artistry of Discussion Leadership.* Boston: Harvard Business School Press, 1991.

Clark, P. "Business Ethics: A Balancing Act." *United Church Observer,* 1994, *57*(7), 18–23.

Cohen, R. *The Good, the Bad and the Difference: How to Tell Right from Wrong in Everyday Situations.* New York: Broadway Books, 2002.

Dalla Costa, J. *The Ethical Imperative: Why Moral Leadership Is Good Business.* Toronto: HarperCollins, 1998.

Dotlich, D., and Cairo, P. *Action Coaching.* San Francisco: Jossey-Bass, 1999.

Garvin, D. A. "A Delicate Balance: Ethical Dilemmas and the Discussion Process." In *Education for Judgment.* Boston: Harvard Business School Press, 1991.

Gaw, B. "Processing Questions: An Aid to Completing the Learning Cycle." In *1979 Annual Handbook for Group Facilitators.* La Jolla, Calif.: University Associates, 1979.

Gaw, B. "Introduction to Structured Experiences." In J. E. Jones and J. W. Pfeiffer (eds.), *1980 Annual Handbook for Group Facilitators.* La Jolla, Calif.: University Associates, 1980.

Gazda, G. M., and others. *Human Relations Development: A Manual for Educators* (3rd ed.). Toronto: Allyn & Bacon, 1984.

Heron, J. *Group Facilitation: Theories and Models for Practice.* London: Kogan Page, 1993.

Hunsaker, P., and Alessandra, A. *The Art of Managing People.* Upper Saddle River, N.J.: Prentice Hall, 1980.

Johnson, D. W., and Johnson, F. P. *Joining Together: Group Theory and Group Skills* (6th ed.). Boston: Allyn & Bacon, 1996.

Jones, J. E., and Pfeiffer, J. W. "Introduction to the Structured Experiences Section." In J. E. Jones and J. W. Pfeiffer (eds.), *1980 Annual Handbook for Group Facilitators.* La Jolla, Calif.: University Associates, 1980.

Kaner, S., and others. *Facilitator's Guide to Participatory Decision-Making.* Gabriola Island, B.C., Canada: New Society, 1996.

Kidney Foundation of Canada. *Advocacy Handbook.* Montreal. [http://www.kidney.ca]. 1999.

Kolb, D. A., and Fry, R. "Towards an Applied Theory of Experiential Learning." In C. L. Cooper (ed.), *Theories of Group Processes.* New York: Wiley, 1975.

Korzybski, A. *Science and Sanity.* International Non-Aristotelian Library. San Francisco: Institute of General Semantics, 1933.

Marks, S., and Davis, W. "The Experiential Learning Model and Its Application to Large Groups." In *1975 Annual Handbook for Group Facilitators.* San Diego: University Associates, 1975.

Metzler, K. *Creative Interviewing: The Writer's Guide to Gathering Information by Asking Questions.* Boston: Allyn & Bacon, 1996.

Michalko, M. *Thinkertoys*. Berkeley, Calif.: Ten Speed Press, 1991.

"Mission, Values, and Vision." [http://www.iaf-world.org]. Mar. 2006.

Moclair, E. "Questionable Experiences in Cambodia." [http://www.cdra.org.za]. Jan. 2002.

Moustakas, C. E. *Finding Yourself, Finding Others*. Upper Saddle River, N.J.: Prentice Hall, 1974.

"Naguib Mahfouz quotes." *ThinkExist.com Quotations Online*. [http://en.thinkexist.com/quotes/naguib_mahfouz/]. 1988.

Nietzsche, F. "There Are No Facts, Only Interpretations." [http://www.quotedb.com/quotes/3311]. Apr. 2006.

Pascale, R. *Managing on the Edge*. New York: Knopf, 1990.

Paul, R., and Elder, L. "Three Categories of Questions: Crucial Distinctions." Dillon Beach, Calif.: Foundation for Critical Thinking [www.criticalthinking.org/resources/articles/crucial-distinctions.shtml]. Oct. 1996.

Payne, S. L. *The Art of Asking Questions*. Princeton: Princeton University Press, 1951.

Peavey, F. *By Life's Grace*. Philadelphia: New Society, 1994.

Peavey, F. "Strategic Questioning." [http://www.cdra.org.za]. Undated.

PEST. [www.marketingteacher.com/Lessons/lesson_PEST.htm]. 2006.

Postman, N., and Weingartner, C. *Teaching as a Subversive Activity*. New York: Delacorte, 1969.

Reddy, W. B. *Intervention Skills: Process Consultation for Small Groups and Teams*. San Diego: Pfeiffer, 1994.

Reinharz, S. "Implementing New Paradigm Research: A Model for Training and Practice." In P. Reason and J. Rowan (eds.), *Human Inquiry*. Toronto: Wiley, 1981.

Roethke, T. "Journey to the Interior." In *The Collected Poems of Theodore Roethke*. Toronto: Doubleday, 1975.

Ross, R., and Roberts, C. "Balancing Inquiry and Advocacy." In P. Senge, A. Kleiner, C. Roberts, R. Ross, and B. Smith, *The Fifth Discipline Fieldbook: Strategies and Tools for Building a Learning Organization*. New York: Currency Doubleday, 1994.

Rowe, M. B. "Wait Time: Slowing Down May Be a Way of Speeding Up." *American Educator,* Spring 1987, *11*, 38–43, 47. (EJ 351 827)

Scholtes, P. *The Leader's Handbook*. Toronto: McGraw-Hill, 1998.

Schön, D. A. *Educating the Reflective Practitioner.* San Francisco: Jossey-Bass, 1987.

Schumacher, E. F. *A Guide for the Perplexed.* New York: HarperCollins, 1977.

Schwarz, R. M. *The Skilled Facilitator.* San Francisco: Jossey-Bass, 1994.

Schwarz, R., and others. *The Skilled Facilitator Fieldbook: Tips, Tools, and Tested Methods for Consultants, Facilitators, Managers, Trainers, and Coaches.* San Francisco: Jossey-Bass, 2005.

Senge, P. *The Fifth Discipline: The Art and Practice of the Learning Organization.* New York: Currency Doubleday, 1990.

Senge, P., and others. *The Fifth Discipline Fieldbook: Strategies and Tools for Building a Learning Organization.* New York: Currency Doubleday, 1994.

Stahl, R. J. *"Using 'Think-Time' and 'Wait-Time' Skillfully in the Classroom" in A to Z Teacher Stuff, Spring Resources.* Bloomington, IN: ERIC Clearinghouse for Social Studies/Social Science Education, May 1994.

Stanfield, R. B. *The Art of Focused Conversation.* Toronto: New Society Publishers, 2000a.

Stanfield, R. B. *The Courage to Lead.* Gabriola Island, B.C., Canada: New Society Publishers, 2000b.

Strachan, D. *Nobody's Perfect Training Manual.* Ottawa, Canada: Federal Government Ministry of Supply and Services, 1988.

Strachan, D., and Pitters, M. *Workshop Management: Method to Magic—A Resource for Facilitators.* Ottawa: National Library of Canada Cataloguing in Publication Data, 2003.

Strachan, D., Shaw, J., Kent, J., and Tomlinson, P. *Volunteers Working Together.* Ottawa, Canada: Skills Program for Volunteers in Recreation, Fitness and Sport, 1986.

Strachan, D., and Tomlinson, P. *Gender Equity in Coaching.* Ottawa: Coaching Association of Canada, 1996.

Sudman, S., and Bradburn, N. M. *Asking Questions: A Practical Guide to Questionnaire Design.* San Francisco: Jossey-Bass, 1982.

"SWOT Analysis: Lesson." [http://www.marketingteacher.com/Lessons/lesson_swot.htm]. 2006.

Szymborska, W. "An Opinion on the Question of Pornography." In *View with a Grain of Sand*. Orlando, Fla.: Harcourt Brace, 1995.

Terry, R. W. *Authentic Leadership: Courage in Action*. San Francisco: Jossey-Bass, 1993.

Tomlinson, P., and Strachan, D. *A Resource Manual for AIDS Educators*. Ottawa: Canadian Public Health Association, 1991.

Tomlinson, P., and Strachan, D. *Power and Ethics in Coaching*. Ottawa: Coaching Association of Canada, 1996.

Tuckman, B. W. "Development Sequence in Small Groups." *Psychological Bulletin,* June 1965, *63,* 384–399.

Weaver, R. G., and Farrell, J. D. *Managers as Facilitators*. San Francisco: Berrett–Koehler, 1997.

Wheeler, M., and Marshall, J. "The Trainer Type Inventory (TTI): Identifying Training Style Preferences." In J. W. Pfeiffer and L. G. Goodstein (eds.), *The 1986 Annual: Developing Human Resources*. San Diego: University Associates, 1986.

CONTINUATION OF COPYRIGHT PAGE